Outside the Lines

Charles K. Ross

Outside the Lines

African Americans and the Integration of the
National Football League

New York University Press • New York and London

NEW YORK UNIVERSITY PRESS
New York and London

© 1999 by New York University

Library of Congress Cataloging-in-Publication Data
Ross, Charles Kenyatta, 1964–
Outside the lines : African Americans and the integration of
the National Football League / Charles K. Ross.
p.   cm.
Includes bibliographical references and index.
ISBN 0-8147-7495-4 (acid-free paper)
1. National Football League—History. 2. Afro-American football
players—Biography. 3. Discrimination in sports—United States—
History.   I. Title.
GV955.5.N35 R67 1999
796.332'64'08996073—dc21   99-6581
                                                                CIP

New York University Press books are printed on acid-free paper,
and their binding materials are chosen for strength and durability.

Manufactured in the United States of America
10 9 8 7 6 5 4 3 2 1

For my family

If I have to integrate heaven, I don't want to go.

—**WOODY STRODE,** during a 1971 interview with *Sports Illustrated* describing his experience with the 1946 LA Rams

Contents

Introduction   1

1   Kickoff: The First Black Pro   3
2   Early Black Pioneers: From Fritz Pollard to
Joe Lillard   21
3   Invisible Men: The NFL Color Barrier   49
4   Reintegration: Washington, Strode, Willis, and
Motley   81
5   First and Ten: The Early Years of Reintegration   99
6   A New League with Old Rules: "The Golden Decade
of the 1950s"   119
7   Touchdown: The Integration of the Washington
Redskins   143

Epilogue: The State of the Game   159

Appendix: African Americans in Pro Football,
1904–1962   165

Notes   179

Bibliography   191

Index   197

About the Author   201

All illustrations appear as a group following p. 108.

Outside the Lines

Introduction

This book began in the spring of 1992 when I was discussing possible dissertation topics with my advisor. He posed the question, "Who was the first black African American professional football player?" I had no idea. Like many, I knew the story of Jackie Robinson breaking the color barrier in major league baseball, but I was completely in the dark regarding the history of blacks in the National Football League. This naturally got me wondering why this story is not widely known. I soon discovered the answer to my advisor's question—it was a black player named Charles Follis—but I also realized that the integration of professional football by black players was a larger story that needed to be chronicled.

Today, 68 percent of the players in the National Football League are African Americans. But I would venture to say that not many are aware of the sacrifice and struggle of men such as Charles Follis, Fritz Pollard, Joe Lillard, Kenny Washington, Bill Willis, Marion Motley, and Bobby Mitchell, who created the opportunities today's players take for granted. Of the major team sports, only professional basketball has a larger percentage of black players. But with the continued increase of black players in pro football, that may soon change.

This account of African American professional football players from 1904 through 1962 seeks to describe and interpret some

central themes of that history: how and why black players were allowed to participate in small numbers in the NFL until 1933; the
creation of the league's color barrier by white owners; the impact
of World War II on the reintegration of the NFL in 1946, together with public pressure generated primarily by the black
press, the creation of a rival league, and the realization of some
white owners and coaches that by using black talent their teams
could realize their ultimate goal—that of winning; and, finally
how the reintegration process visibly changed professional football by 1962. However, these central themes are themselves but a
part of two larger subjects in American history: the development
of leisure and sporting activity in American life after the Civil
War; and the socioeconomic impact of this development in relation to the sport of professional football and race relations
through the heyday of the modern civil rights movement.

Like most other American social, political, and economic institutions, sports were racially restrictive or segregated in accor-
dance with the doctrine of "separate and equal" as manifested in
the 1896 *Plessy* decision. However, the playing fields of America
were integrated years before the Supreme Court reversed itself in
1954. In many ways sports set the tone for America to begin integration off the field. The NFL was the first major sport to lower
its color barrier during the postwar period, though not without a
struggle. This work thus serves as a forceful reminder of the contributions and sacrifices made by black players in the past.

1. Kickoff

The First Black Pro

Late-nineteenth-century America witnessed many societal changes, one of which was the widespread obsession with sport. The growth of the American sporting scene began at midcentury and then accelerated after the Civil War, primarily as a result of urbanization and industrialization. However, not all Americans were able to participate in this newly growing sporting experience. As America embraced formal legal segregation by the end of the century, the eviction of African Americans from many professional sports was already under way. The color barrier became the universal rule adopted for African Americans, despite their clearly outstanding and in many cases superior skills in various sports.[1]

African Americans were involved in all the major late-nineteenth and early-twentieth-century popular sports, ranging from horse racing, baseball, bicycling, to boxing and football. Black jockeys dominated their profession from roughly 1800 until the eve of World War I. In 1875, the first year of the Kentucky Derby, thirteen of the fourteen jockeys were black. African American jockeys won eleven of the first twenty Kentucky Derbys. Isaac Murphy, the most famous black jockey in 1893, earned around $250,000 in winnings over the course of the year and was paid roughly $10,000. Murphy's winning record of 44 percent is a feat yet to be equaled. But in 1894 the Jockey Club was formed to license riders; it immediately began to systematically deny the enlistment of blacks. Subsequently, by the first decade of the twentieth century the black jockey was virtually extinct.

In baseball, J. W. "Bud" Fowler, the first known full-time black professional, began playing in 1872 with Evansville. He played through 1879 with several teams. Moses Fleetwood Walker and his brother Weldy Walker both played major league baseball for one year in 1884 with Toledo of the American Association. But the widening patterns of racial segregation in America facilitated the end of black participation in major and minor league baseball by 1889. Cyclist Marshall "Major" Taylor has the distinction of being the first African American to win a national title in any sport. During the 1890s Taylor earned as much as $20,000 a year. In 1898 the American Racing Cyclists' Union was formed and barred all blacks from membership. Taylor was forced to finish his career in Europe and Australia, where he went on to set world records in the quarter-mile sprint in 1908.[2]

Heavyweight champion Jack Johnson has traditionally been considered the first major black sports figure in American life. His social lifestyle outside the ring, specifically his open fraternization with white women, and his athletic exploits inside the ring, knocking out white opponents relatively easily, played on white America's greatest fears. Clearly Johnson represented dangerous possibilities to white America regarding black athletes in general. In Jim Crow America, Johnson set the tone for the controversial role African Americans could and might play in the sporting world if full racial integration were allowed. So by 1915 the black athlete had been effectively banned from all the major professional sports. During the first three decades of the twentieth century professional football was not a widely supported sport and labored in local obscurity. However, arguably it was this obscurity that allowed limited black participation. Only seventeen blacks played professional football from 1904 until 1933.

Unlike baseball, the football season was too short and the gate receipts too meager to make pro football anything like a career occupation. Many players held full-time jobs in industry and played on Sundays for the joy of it and to supplement their incomes. The blue-collar orientation of the game seems significant in explaining the long-standing hostility or apathy toward the game by leading newspapers, university officials, and a large segment of the public. It was against this backdrop that a few black players were given the opportunity to play professionally. With a small fan base, the game and players were largely unknown to many Americans. This relative obscurity created playing opportunities for a few select black players. However, once professional football began to gain popularity and established itself firmly as a major American sport, black players were soon ousted from the game.

Professional football evolved from local athletic clubs which traced their beginnings to college football, a very popular student activity. In 1869 Princeton and Rutgers played the first intercollegiate football game in the United States. Harvard and Yale played their inaugural game in 1875; and the next year four Ivy League institutions formed the Intercollegiate Football Association to standardize rules. Harvard's rugby school style of play won out over Yale's soccer style, and before long new rules added such familiar features as blocking, alternating ball possessions, fixed numbers of downs, and other hallmarks of the American game. By the 1880s and 1890s, football was a central feature of college social life. While there were other college sports, football came to stand for them all. But the game itself, the way it was played, especially the style and specific rules, can be credited to one man—Walter Camp.[3]

Walter Camp, "the father of American football," was an outstanding player at Yale and a genius at developing plans for attack. His football career began at Yale in 1876. After graduating in 1880, he stayed on for two years as a medical student and continued to play football. It was in 1880 that he devised one of the most far-reaching rule changes in the history of the sport. The new rule, establishing the line of scrimmage, began to transform English rugby into American football. Two years later, again under Camp's leadership, came the series of downs to gain a set number of yards (initially five), new styles of blocking (or interference, as it was known at the time), and tackles below the waist.[4]

In 1889 Camp was the first to name an All-America team, commonly called the Walter Camp All-America. Over the years he selected a number of black players. One of the men Camp selected for the 1892 and 1893 teams was center William Henry Lewis, who was the first black college player and first black All-American.[5]

The son of free mulatto blacks before the Civil War, Lewis was born in Berkeley, Virginia, on November 28, 1868. After graduating from Virginia Normal and Industrial, Lewis enrolled at Amherst College in 1888 at the suggestion of Virginia Normal's president, John Langston. Lewis felt strongly that he must prove that blacks were "fit," and that he had the equipment to prove it. Not only was he an outstanding scholar, selected as orator for the class of 1892, but he was also a superb athlete. He played football for four years at Amherst and was captain of the Amherst team during the 1891 season. Lewis became the first "roving lineman" in the game. A good-sized man for the times—five feet eleven inches, 177 pounds—he played in an era when helmets were not used, and he opposed the idea of free substitutions, allowing only unconsciousness or delirium as a reason for replacement.[6]

After graduating from Amherst, Lewis enrolled in law school at Harvard, where he continued to play football. In his first game for Harvard in 1892, he helped defeat Dartmouth 48–0. But against archrival Yale before twenty thousand fans—then the largest crowd ever to watch a black athlete in a team sport—Harvard lost to Yale 6–0. However, Walter Camp was in attendance and named Lewis to his All-America team at center-rush for 1892, making Lewis the first black player to be so honored. Lewis's outstanding play continued the following season and Camp made him a repeat selection in 1893.[7]

However, as Lewis and other black players integrated white institutions, African Americans were losing their legal rights as citizens. In 1878, the Supreme Court declared unconstitutional a Louisiana statute banning discrimination in transportation. In 1882, the Court voided the Ku Klux Klan Act of 1871, deciding that the civil rights protections of the Fourteenth Amendment applied to states rather than to individuals. In 1883, the provisions of the Civil Rights Act of 1875, which assured blacks equal rights in public places, were declared unconstitutional. By the 1890s, state and local laws had legalized informal segregation in public facilities. The Supreme Court upheld these laws in 1896 in *Plessy v. Ferguson* by declaring that "separate but equal" facilities did not violate the equal protection clause of the Fourteenth Amendment. Against this backdrop several black players participated on white college teams.

William Tecumseh Sherman Jackson was the second African American to play college football. A teammate of Lewis at Amherst in 1890, Jackson was a solid halfback. The third and fourth black players to enter the college game also made their debuts in 1890. George Jeweth was a punter, field-goal kicker, and halfback at the University of Michigan. William Arthur Johnson played halfback at the Massachusetts Institute of Technology. At the University of Nebraska, George A. Flippin starred at halfback from 1892 to 1894. William Lee Washington lettered at Oberlin as a halfback from 1895 to 1897. More than fifty black players played on white college teams from 1889 through 1920. However, seldom were there more than two blacks on one team. And most white schools had no black players at all.[8]

During the age of legal segregation African Americans had few opportunities to enroll at white universities, let alone participate on their football teams. Nevertheless, blacks saw education as a key factor that could help them elevate themselves, and this responsibility fell upon historically black colleges and universities. Like their white counterparts, historically black colleges and universities founded their own teams. Pennsylvania's Cheyney State, founded in 1837, was the oldest and one of only three black colleges in existence prior to the Civil War. Lincoln (Pennsylvania) and Wilberforce (Ohio) universities were the other two, founded in 1854 and 1856 respectively.[9]

Black colleges did not share in the football craze because of poor facilities and lack of money. School administrators were not willing to spend any of their already meager funds on games. However, as the schools began to grow, many presidents began to see the need for physical education programs, and from many of those programs intramural football teams were formed with students as coaches. The lack of enthusiasm for football at black colleges reversed itself on December 27, 1892, in a Salisbury, North Carolina, cow pasture. There, in a snowstorm, Biddle College (now Johnson C. Smith) took on and defeated home team Livingstone College, 4-0, marking the first intercollegiate football game between historically black schools. A friendly rivalry, as well as an athletic history for an entire race, had begun.[10]

Traditional football rivalries between black colleges continued through the twentieth century and became stronger as football became more popular. Both Howard and Lincoln universities, the Tuskegee Institute, and Atlanta University first played in 1894; and Howard University and Morgan College played in 1899 on the Howard campus. These rivalries fostered community pride and still endure today.

Commercialism in football became inevitable as the interest of students, social climbing alumni, and college authorities grew. This growing popularity was not confined to colleges. During the last third of the nineteenth century, new industrial elites became fascinated with sports, and they joined together in a variety of exclusive athletic organizations. The founding of the New York Athletic Club in 1866 marked the single most important step in this movement. Similar metropolitan clubs quickly proliferated. There were one hundred and fifty by 1883, and many promoted elaborate annual athletic meets. These athletic clubs made it possible to enjoy recreational pursuits within congested cities. As college players entered the business world in the various towns and cities of the East and Midwest, they introduced football into athletic clubs. In the state of Pennsylvania, professional football spread from such clubs in and around Pittsburgh to the surrounding mining and mill towns. These clubs began to play each other, and local loyalty to the teams developed.[11]

When exactly football became truly professional is difficult to determine. The practice of players receiving trophies that could be readily exchanged for cash was quite common. For example, in the early 1890s, one New York City athletic club gave its players a gold watch as a "trophy" after each game. Players then took the watch to a designated shop and pawned it for roughly $20. This was done so the player and club could avoid the wrath of the Amateur Athletic Union which could punish violators of the amateur code by banning them from competition with "honest" AAU members.

It was within this environment of "amateurism" that the first player was paid cash for his play. The city of Pittsburgh was the site of an intense rivalry between two athletic clubs, the Pittsburgh Athletic Club (PAC) and the Allegheny Athletic Association (AAA). On November 12, 1892, Pudge Heffelfinger, a three-time All-America guard from Yale, became the first known professional football player. Heffelfinger was secretly handed $500 to play for the AAA against archrival PAC. A week after the "Heffelfinger game," the AAA paid former Princeton end Sport Donnelly, one of Heffelfinger's friends, $250 to play against Washington and Jefferson. Despite the presence of the second known pro, the AAA lost. In 1893, the AAA paid Pete Wright, James Van Cleve, and Ollie Rafferty $50 each per game.[12] As payments to individual players became prevalent, compensation for an entire team followed naturally. In Latrobe, Westmoreland County, Pennsylvania, a local YMCA sponsored a team that on August 31, 1895, defeated another team from nearby Jeannette by a score of 12-0. The Latrobe team stayed together and for the next ten years played wherever they could find an opponent for whatever money they could get. And thus professional football began to take hold.

Although pro football was born in Pennsylvania, it was in Ohio that the game matured. In 1901 the number of Ohio amateur athletic clubs playing football increased dramatically. Akron developed several intracity rivalries, as the South End Athletic Club and the Planet Athletic Club joined the North End Athletic Club in fielding teams. Other cities and towns, including Lorain, Steubenville, Newark, Barberton, and Zanesville also played organized football. And in 1902 the Shelby (Ohio) Athletic Club was recognized by local newspapers as a professional team. By now the formation of another professional team was not necessarily news, but Shelby AC's inclusion of a black player on its roster was.[13]

Charles W. Follis became football's first black professional when he signed to play for the Shelby Athletic Club on September 15, 1904. (Although Follis had played the two previous years, 1904 was the first year in which he received documented compensation.) Follis, one of seven children, was born in Cloverdale near Roanoke, Virginia, on February 3, 1879. The family migrated to Wooster, Ohio, when Follis was quite young. His football career began in 1899, when he helped Wooster High School officials organize a varsity program. He was the team's first captain—and right halfback. Wooster scored 122 points that season, its opponents zero.[14]

Follis entered the College of Wooster in the spring of 1901. That fall he did not play football for the college, but for the Wooster Athletic Association, a local amateur team. So great were his efforts with the Wooster AA that he became known as the "Black Cyclone from Wooster." The team wasn't much. It lost to Shelby 5-0 in one game and was then beaten again 28-5 by the same team. But after seeing Follis play, manager Frank Schiffer persuaded him to join his Shelby team in 1902. Schiffer secured a job for Follis at Howard Seltzer and Sons Hardware Store, where his working hours were arranged so that he could practice and play football. His presence caused a few waves in the rural white community. In fact, he was something of a curiosity as a store clerk. People dropped by Seltzer's as much to see and talk with Follis as to shop.[15]

Although Follis had exceptional football skills, his baseball abilities were perhaps even stronger. He became the talk of the Ohio college baseball circuit largely because of his tremendous power hitting. While catching for Wooster Follis first met Branch Rickey, then playing for Ohio Wesleyan University. Follis was a man of great pride. Although he was the frequent target of verbal and physical abuse from white fans and opponents, even on the most trying occasions he never resorted to belligerent behavior or open hostility. Follis's attitude appears to have left a lasting impression on Rickey. He later required Jackie Robinson to adopt a similar strategy of tolerating racial abuse while breaking the color barrier in major league baseball.[16]

Charles Follis was a 1902 and 1903 teammate of Branch Rickey on the Shelby Athletic Club team. In 1903, Follis had one of his best amateur days against an all-Cleveland team. Shelby won 16-0, with Follis running 70 yards for a touchdown. Because he was a star and because he was black, Follis became a target for the opposition, which was not accustomed to playing against an integrated opponent. In 1903, for instance, the Marion team went after Follis in the hope of putting him out of the game. As the *Shelby Globe* reported, "Marion's quarterback started dirty work on Follis and . . . Dave Bushey, his teammate, interceded and acted as policeman." Marion's efforts were for naught: Shelby won 40-0. In the next game Follis ran 20, 25, 35, and 70 yards against Rickey's Ohio Wesleyan team—without incident. But in a 22-5 victory over the Columbus Panhandles, Follis was roughed up, suffering torn shoulder ligaments.[17]

Follis turned professional on September 15, 1904, yet his signing received only a few lines in the *Globe*: "The Shelby Athletic Association has secured the services of Charles Follis for this season. The contract has been signed and football enthusiasts will be pleased to know Follis will be on the local team again this year. Follis plays halfback and there is no better in the state."[18] There is no record of what Follis received in dollars and cents for his football services; players who received pay did so after the hat was passed in the stands. The signing of Follis in 1904, though he had played for two previous years, was tied directly to the success of the Massillon Tigers. In 1903 Massillon hired four veteran pros from Pittsburgh to help them win the Ohio state football championship from Akron. The next year saw at least eight Ohio teams paying players on a more or less regular basis, including the Shelby AC.

Follis's first game as a professional came eight days after his signing, against Marion. He was superb, guiding Shelby to a 29-0 victory with an 83–yard touchdown run. In game two, Shelby kicked off to the Brooklyn Athletic Club of Cleveland, which promptly fumbled. Shelby recovered on the four–yard line. Follis went in for the touchdown, and kicked the extra point. Shelby was on the way to a 53-0 win. Fast on the heels of that one-sided beating came a 48-0 victory over the Akron Imperials; a 27-0 win over Lorain; and a 29-0 win over the Akron Deaf Mutes. In a showdown with powerful Massillon, Follis didn't play the first half. Some said he was hurt. Some said it was a psychological ploy, but if it was it backfired, as Massillon won 28-0. Shelby went on to three more easy victories and in ten games, scored 317 points— and gave up only the 28 points to Massillon. Follis's remarkable 1904 season had intensified the desire of Shelby's opponents— and their fans—to remove him from action. They used words, knuckles, and knees. The team kept winning, but Follis was paying a heavy price physically and emotionally.[19]

In a November 1905 game against Toledo, player and fan abuse toward Follis mounted. From his right halfback position, Follis had been making the day miserable for Toledo players. According to the *Toledo Evening News Bee* on November 29, 1905:

> Follis, the Shelby halfback, is a Negro and the crowd got after him, advising the local players to put him out of the game. Toledo captain Jack Tattersoll stopped the game and yelled to the crowd: "Don't call Follis a nigger. He is a gentleman and a clean player and please don't call him that." He [Tattersoll] was applauded for his sentiment and the colored player was not molested during the remainder of the game.[20]

Frequent injuries, and infrequent intervention like that of Toledo's Tattersoll, eventually took an apparent toll on Follis. He was a key figure in 1906 as Schiffer announced plans to turn the amateur Shelby Athletic Club into a professional team, which he did by forming the Shelby Blues. For a reason never announced,

Follis didn't play in the Blues' first three games, but he was there in a 58-0 loss to Massillon, and for three victories that followed. On Thanksgiving day 1906, in a game versus Franklin Athletic Club, Shelby played to a 0-0 tie. But more significantly, this was the last known football appearance of Charles W. Follis. Near the end of the game, he was helped off the field with a leg injury.[21]

Follis's efforts were appreciated by his teammates and the club's loyal fans, but the acceptance was far from unanimous. After one particularly rugged practice session, the Blues crowded into a Shelby tavern for refreshments. At a teammate's urging, Follis went along, for the first—and last—time. The tavern owner saw him and announced that only the white football players could stay. Black ones would have to go. He left, choosing to take his refreshment alone. That was his way. He was a frequent loner, sometimes by choice, but more often because of social pressures.[22]

After the end of his football career Follis began playing professional black baseball, ending up with the Cuban Giants, where he played successfully until his early death in 1910, at the age of thirty-one. In a 1975 interview his sister-in-law, Florence Follis, recalled that after a postgame shower Follis sat on the porch of his Cleveland home for a couple of hours before beginning to shake; he was rushed to a local hospital where he died of pneumonia. Buried in Wooster Cemetery in a grave marked by a thin weathered headstone, Follis has never been given the historic recognition for his contribution in professional football, but has remained hidden, much as his grave is during the winter by drifting Ohio snow.

In 1906, the year Follis hung up his cleats, the second black pro made his debut; Charles "Doc" Baker played halfback for the Akron Indians. He was on the squad from 1906 to 1908, mysteriously left for two years, and then returned in 1911. Like Follis, Baker was the target of the opposing team's constant attempts to injure him. However, unlike Follis, Baker suffered through no fault of his own from several gambling scandals that rocked professional football from 1906 to 1911. Betting on games was furious, and after the Canton Bulldogs were charged with throwing the 1906 game against archrival Massillon, fans began to stay away. As a result many teams found it difficult to pay their players, and Baker seems to have left professional football for this reason.[23]

The first major scandal in the history of professional football occurred in 1906. It centered on the fever-pitch intercity rivalry between the Canton Bulldogs and the Massillon Tigers, both from Ohio. Canton's team was formed the previous year, primarily to beat Massillon. The two cities, both in Stark County, were traditional rivals. Each scrambled to hire the best players in the county in the hope of becoming Ohio state champs. Massillon had defeated Canton in their first meeting, 14–4. The championship was decided in 1905 when the teams had their second meeting, but there was some controversy. Massillon was owned by a city newspaper editor, and it was he who provided a ten-ounce school ball for the game instead of the regulation sixteen-ounce one used by the professionals. When Massillon won the game 10-0, Blondy Wallace, the Canton coach, protested vigorously, but to no avail. So he retaliated by recruiting the whole Massillon starting backfield for the next season.[24]

The next year Wallace, with a new backfield, beat Massillon 10-5 in the first game of a two-game series. The Bulldogs were naturally favorites for the second meeting, to be held in Massillon. However, Massillon kept its championship, with a 13-6 win in the rematch. But shortly after the second game a Massillon newspaper charged Wallace with throwing the game. Canton insisted Massillon simply wanted to cripple the Bulldogs financially by destroying the gate for their remaining games with Latrobe. Massillon couldn't prove its charge but the stands were virtually empty for the Canton-Latrobe game and the Bulldogs couldn't pay their players. The scandal almost stopped professional football in its tracks. It would be a full decade before the fledgling sport recovered.[25]

As the legacy of the Massillon-Canton scandal began to fade, the third black professional player entered the game. He was Haitian-born Henry McDonald, born on August 31, 1890, in Port-au-Prince. McDonald was brought to America when very young and adopted by a Canandigua, New York, family. A running back for the Oxford (New York) Pros in 1911 and then for the Rochester Jeffersons in 1912, he earned $25 per game. McDonald spent seven seasons with the Jeffersons and was nicknamed "the Motorcycle." McDonald's last year of professional action was 1920, but in 1917 he played against the incomparable Jim Thorpe. Although Thorpe's Canton team won 49-0, the game and Thorpe left a lasting impression on McDonald.[26]

McDonald, a peppery eighty-year-old in 1971, recalled that he had experienced racial unpleasantness on the field only once. Playing for the Jeffersons in a game against Canton in 1917, Marshall attempted to tackle the Bulldogs' Greasy Neale, who promptly shoved him out of bounds, cocked his fist, and shouted, "Black is black and white is white, and where I come from they don't mix." According to McDonald, Jim Thorpe prevented a donnybrook when he jumped between the two players and said, "We're here to play football." McDonald related that "Thorpe's word was law on the field" and he never had any problem after that.[27]

This particular incident was simply a microcosm of what African Americans encountered during this golden age of segregation. For Follis, Baker, and McDonald racial prejudice on and off the field was simply the American way of life. The opportunity to play a physical sport such as football with and against white players was an accomplishment in itself for early black pros. Physical and verbal abuse were just consequences that came with the territory. But these three black athletes weren't alone in challenging Jim Crow America by their on-the-field existence. They were joined by one of the greatest boxers of all time—Jack Johnson.

When Johnson won the heavyweight championship in 1908, he provided African Americans with a shot of racial pride and left an indelible bad taste in the mouth of white America. Johnson played on America's greatest fears regarding black inferiority and interracial relationships—but maybe it was how he did it rather than what he did that caused him to be feared. Johnson played on white fears purposely. From open consorting with white women to torturing his white opponents, he relished the negative perceptions of white Americans. Both blacks and whites alike recognized that during this era his habit of whipping white men in the ring was a political act of far-reaching dimensions. When Johnson defeated Jim Jefferies, the "Great White Hope," on July 4, 1910, whites attacked blacks in riots that spread across America. Arguably it was better for Johnson to have won and a few blacks killed in body than for Johnson to have lost and many blacks been killed in spirit. So when Johnson lost the heavyweight championship to Jess Willard in 1915 as a result of a controversial knockout, white America let out a grateful sigh of relief.

For African Americans 1915 was a dreadful year. Woodrow Wilson, the first southern-born president since the Civil War, was in the process of implementing his executive order segregating black employees in their workplaces. The wartime migration of southern blacks to northern cities had created tremendous competition for jobs. The movie director D. W. Griffith released his blatantly racist film *The Birth of a Nation,* which sparked the NAACP to lead black protests against its showing across the country. In Alabama, Colonel William J. Simmons revived the Ku

Klux Klan, touching off numerous incidents of racial violence. It was reported that fifty-six blacks were lynched during the year. And in November, Booker T. Washington died, leaving a vacuum in black leadership that was difficult to fill.

It was in this environment of growing segregation that the fourth black player was given an opportunity to play professionally. As was the custom in the early days, college athletes often played a game or two with a professional team under an assumed name. Evidence points to the fact that "Charlie" Smith was in fact, Gideon E. Smith, a black athlete who played for the Canton Bulldogs in 1915. Smith was born in Northwest County, Virginia, on July 13, 1889. Eventually becoming professor of physical education at Hampton Institute, he had graduated from that school in 1910. Smith then attended Ferris Institute in Big Rapids, Michigan. He later entered what was then Michigan Agricultural College (now Michigan State University), graduating in 1916.[28]

Smith played only once for the Canton Bulldogs during the 1915 season. John Cussack, coach of the Bulldogs, described his acquisition of Smith for the game of November 28, 1915, against the Massillon Tigers: "I bolstered the Bulldogs with the addition of Charlie Smith, a fine tackle from the Michigan Aggies."[29] There is no evidence that Gideon Smith went on to play any more seasons of professional football, making him the last black to play professional football before the formation of the American Professional Football Association in 1920.

Professional football was a new and relatively minor sport compared to baseball, boxing, and college football. From 1900 to 1920 it suffered from numerous internal problems—the refusal of teams to organize and abide by uniform rules, the unscrupulous raiding of talent from other teams and even colleges, the turnover of players, betting and gambling scandals, and uneven competition. Formal organization was obviously needed. Ironically, for the four black players of the pre-NFL era, this lack of formal organization probably created the environment that allowed them to participate.

Pro football had a long way to go before it could escape the stigma of blatant commercialism, exploitation, and internal bickering. The increasing hostility of college coaches toward the professional game also had a negative impact. But as college football began to regain its popularity and respect after the number of deaths (113 fatalities between 1905 and 1910) declined, so too did professional football. However, unlike college football, pro football lacked formal organization. Pro football yearned for respectability and fan acceptance, and both became realities after the creation of a permanent league.[30]

At the end of World War I, some teams hoped to capitalize on the game's popularity by forming the APFA. In 1920, George Halas, manager, coach, and player of the Staley Starchmakers, wrote a letter to Ralph Hay, manager of the Canton Bulldogs, suggesting that some of the better football teams get together and form a league. On September 17, 1920, managers of eleven professional clubs met in the showroom of Hay's Automobile Agency in Canton, Ohio, to discuss Halas's suggestion. The APFA was formed at this meeting. Jim Thorpe was elected president and eleven franchises were awarded at a cost of $100 each: Canton Bulldogs, Cleveland Indians, Dayton Triangles, Akron Professionals, Massillon Tigers, Rochester All-Stars, Rock Island Independents, Muncie Tigers, Decatur Staleys, Hammond Pros, and Chicago Cardinals. (Only two of the original eleven franchises are still active in the National Football League: the Chicago Bears, formerly known as the Decatur Staleys, and the Arizona Cardinals, formerly called the Chicago Cardinals.)

On June 24, 1922, the APFA was renamed the National Football League. During the next eleven years, the NFL evolved from small-town franchises to urban franchises. The National Football

League consisted of professional, semiprofessional, and amateur football teams. The number of active franchises fluctuated from year to year with a high of twenty-two in 1926 and an all-time low of eight in 1932.

Black player participation in the NFL, as in the various franchises, fluctuated from year to year as well. Professional football struggled to gain acceptance as a national sport during its early days. Without major fan support, a few black players were tolerated and played on various teams, probably in the hope of helping to generate fan interest.

Although the four black football pioneers of the pre-NFL era—Follis, Baker, McDonald, and Smith—have been virtually forgotten, their participation gave several other black athletes opportunities. Thirteen blacks played in the NFL before the creation of the color barrier, a barrier created after the NFL reorganized in 1933 and had begun to establish itself as a major sport. Although discrimination limited the opportunities for black players, from the time of Follis until the color ban their contributions to the development of professional football must not be forgotten.

2. Early Black Pioneers

From Fritz Pollard to Joe Lillard

The summer of 1919 ushered in the greatest period of interracial strife America had ever witnessed. From June to the end of the year dozens of race riots crisscrossed the land. African Americans had adopted a new, more aggressive posture in defense of their rights, an attitude fostered by World War I. The revival of the Ku Klux Klan, which began at the end of the war, also contributed to the growing racial friction. This new Klan came forth with a broad program for "uniting native-born white Christians for concerted action in the preservation of American institutions and the supremacy of the white race." Cells of the organization flourished in several New England states, as well as in New York, Indiana, Illinois, Michigan, and other northern and midwestern states. It was in this atmosphere of anxiety and high racial tension that the black player gradually disappeared from the NFL after the 1926 season.

From 1919 to 1933 only thirteen black players played on professional football teams. When the APFA began play in 1920 the fourteen teams averaged twenty players each. There were only two black players in the league that year, Fritz Pollard of the Akron Pros and Robert Marshall of the Rock Island Independents. Pollard's forced retirement in 1926 signaled the decline of African American participation in professional football before

World War II. During that season a total of thirty-one professional teams were divided between the newly formed and short-lived American Football League and NFL. By 1926 the average team roster consisted of twenty-five players. However, from 1922 through 1926 only nine blacks played for NFL or AFL teams. During the 1927 season Duke Slater of the Chicago Cardinals was the only black player on an NFL roster, until Harold Bradley joined the league in 1928. Bradley was not resigned in 1929 and again Slater was the only black player in the NFL. Only three other blacks played in the league before the color line was drawn in 1933.

The decline of black players in the NFL occurred after the financially disastrous 1926 campaign which caused the subsequent withdrawal of many teams. While twenty-two teams began the 1926 season, only twelve competed for the championship the following year. Jay Williams, Sol Butler, and Dick Hudson played for teams that dropped out of the NFL and were not signed by other franchises. While there is no evidence of an organized racial barrier, it is clear that some teams, such as Hammond and Canton which ceased in 1926, were more willing to hire black players than others. But there is evidence that racial tensions were becoming strained in the NFL by the mid-1920s. For example, on November 5, 1926, New York Giants players refused to take the field in a game against Canton at the Polo Grounds. Giants management maintained that the large crowd might object to the presence of Canton's Sol Butler on the field. The protest could have been linked to a number of southern players on the New York team. After a ten-minute delay, Butler withdrew voluntarily, advising his teammates to play and not disappoint the crowd.[1]

Aside from the prevailing racial climate, a number of factors made it difficult for African Americans to find employment in the NFL. The most obvious was the small number of blacks who played football at white colleges, which were the recruiting grounds for professional teams. Beyond that, most black players had to achieve All-America status just to be considered by the pro teams. Apparently the increasing acceptance of professional football by the fans during the 1920s allowed owners to release African American players who had earlier been needed as drawing cards. Major black newspapers, moreover, rarely covered the professional game, and its following in the African American community was limited. As a rule, black fans, like white fans, did not have as much faith in professional football as they did in the college game. Under these circumstances, pro football owners had little incentive to hire African American players unless they were clearly superior and could assure victories.[2]

Robert W. Marshall and Fritz Pollard were the first two blacks to play in the newly formed APFA of 1920. Unlike Pollard who became the NFL's first black star, Marshall did not get the opportunity to play until the twilight of his football career. Not listed as a full professional, "Bobby" or "Rube" Marshall played semiprofessional ball from 1906 through 1919. Born on March 12, 1880, he was an end on the University of Minnesota football teams of 1904 to 1906. Starting as a substitute player in 1903, he was selected to Walter Camp's prestigious All-American teams in 1905 and 1906. In Marshall's three years on the Minnesota varsity, the team won twenty-five games and lost two. After graduating from the University of Minnesota, Marshall played semipro football for several years before entering the NFL. His NFL career included membership on the Rock Island Independents from 1919 to 1920 and Duluth Kelleys in 1925. He ended his brief NFL career with Duluth, still playing end at age forty-five![3]

Fritz Pollard's career stands in stark contrast to Marshall's brief, obscure stint. In the early 1920s the new National Football League needed star performers to enable it to compete with the college game. Pollard was born in Rogers Park, a suburb of Chicago, in 1894. He was an All-American at Brown University and an ideal drawing card for the new league. His father owned a barber shop, and had been a champion boxer during the Civil War. In an interview given later in his life, Pollard recalled his family's participation in sports:

> I had an older brother, Luther J., who was an outstanding athlete and football player at Lakeview High School and Northwestern University way back in the nineties. Then I had another brother named Leslie, who was a great football player at Dartmouth. Later he became coach and athletic director at Lincoln University. I had another brother named Hughes who was the reason I got a chance to play football at our high school, Lane Tech in Chicago. He was the big shot on the team and he told the coach if his kid brother couldn't play, he wouldn't play either. I weighed all of eighty-nine pounds. But as the years went by, I became the star of the team.[4]

In 1913 Pollard registered at Northwestern University near his home, but was told to leave when the dean found out that he just wanted to play football. Then, in February 1914 Pollard applied to Brown. Having gone to a technical high school, he still did not have sufficient foreign language credits for admission to Brown as a regular student. He then tried Dartmouth, where his brother had played, but was not admitted because he had been less than candid about attempting to enter Brown University. On to Harvard, where he suited up but sat on the bench during a game against Bates College. Then he tried Bates but left because Maine was too cold. Finally his friends persuaded him to earn the proper credits for admission to Brown. In the fall of 1915 he entered Brown as a twenty-one-year-old freshman.[5] According to Pollard:

This came about after I went East to New York with Lane Tech to play a high school game. The Rockefellers (John D., in particular), who were Brown University people, took an interest in me after they saw me play ball. I talked with him and it was decided that I would go to Brown in Providence, Rhode Island. I was the first black man to live on the campus. The Rockefellers paid my tuition, so they had to let me live there.

The captain of the Brown team was the star quarterback, Clair Purdy. We were freshmen together. He paved the way for me socially and on the football field. He fought off all the objections that came over my playing on the team. He used to say if I couldn't play, he wouldn't play. But let's not forget the Rockefeller family were great supporters of the school, so I could overcome a lot of nonsense. It made things easier.

Playing football for Brown was rough. They'd call me "nigger" from the stands. . . . "Kill the nigger! Don't let him do that!" was all I heard. That was the first year. Then things started working out.[6]

At the end of Pollard's freshman season Brown finished with a record of five wins, three losses, and one tie. Mostly on the basis of its victory over Yale, the first since 1910, Brown appeared in the Rose Bowl on January 1, 1916. However, as Pollard described it, bowl officials were less than enthusiastic about his participation: "It was January 1, 1916, when they invited Brown to the coast to play Washington State in the Tournament of Roses; later they called it the Rose Bowl. Nothing was said at first, but then the bowl game officials and everybody else said they didn't want the nigger to play, meaning me, of course, but our team and manager refused to play unless I played, so everything was alright."[7] However, the field was a quagmire because of a torrential rainstorm which greatly curtailed Pollard's running ability, and Washington State won 14-0. During the game Pollard was tackled in what Coach Edward "Robbie" Robinson described as a four inch-deep puddle, causing him to fear that by the time the players unpiled Pollard may have drowned. Shortly after this Pollard was removed from the game, but kept leaving the bench begging to be put back in. Interestingly, Pollard recounted that years later he met Walt Disney who had been at the game and never forgot the image of Pollard continually jumping off the bench attempting to reenter the game. Pollard attributed this image to Disney's creation of a cartoon where Mickey Mouse continuously attempts to reenter a game against a team of Lions, pleading: "Put me in, please, Coach, put me in."[8]

During Pollard's second season, on October 28, 1916 Brown faced Rutgers University. Opposite Pollard stood a man who would become his friend for life, Paul Robeson, who like Pollard was the only black player on his team. Brown, led by Pollard's two touchdowns, defeated Rutgers 21-3. At the end of the season Pollard was named to Walter Camp's All-America team as the left halfback. Camp called Pollard "the most elusive back of the year or of any year." Pollard became the second African American named to the Walter Camp first team All-America squad, and the first to be selected for a backfield position.[9]

Being named to Walter Camp's All-America team changed Pollard's life dramatically in both the short and long term. Reflecting on the honor more than fifty years later, Pollard said, "Having been placed on the All American team by Walter Camp helped me all through my life. Having been the first Negro backfield man to have been given the honor. It helped me in business because people trusted me and I had to live within that trust. It gave me recognition wherever I went and cleared the way for me many times when otherwise I would have been very much embarrassed."[10]

The immediate effects of his selection were quite overwhelming for the young Pollard. As he recalled, "I began receiving invitations from all over the country to make speeches." During the Christmas recess and well into the second semester, Pollard remembered speaking "in Chicago, Philadelphia, Pittsburgh, Washington D.C. and Baltimore and many other places especially New York where the NAACP held a very large reception for me as did the other places." During the spring semester of 1917, Pollard's fame caused him to be engaged in a large number of campus and off-campus activities, which consumed a good deal of his time. And eventually they took their toll on him academically. However, on April 2 America plunged into war.[11]

For many African Americans the war presented a dilemma. With the majority of blacks relegated to second-class citizenship, support for the Allied cause varied in the black community both before and after America's declaration of war. Some black newspapers such as the *Washington Bee*, the *Iowa Bystander*, and the *Chicago Defender* opposed American intervention and the participation of black soldiers if war came. *The Messenger*, a labor publication edited by A. Philip Randolph and Chandler Owen, suggested that flag-waving leaders in the African American community should "volunteer to go on to France, if they are so eager to make the world safe for democracy. We would rather fight to make Georgia safe for the Negro." Many black leaders, however, and particularly those associated with the NAACP and the National Urban League, supported American intervention and African American participation in the war effort. W. E. B. Du Bois, editor of the NAACP's publication, the *Crisis*, played a leading role in mobilizing black support for the war. Du Bois, after agonizing over his position, convinced himself that, given the opposition even to black enlisted men, the commissioning of black officers in whatever circumstances was imperative. Still, he wondered why "cannot the nation that has absorbed ten million foreigners . . . absorb ten million Negro Americans . . . ? Pained, Du Bois accepted the absurd logic of having to fight "even to be segregated."[12] And once it became clear that African Americans would be drafted, most of the black press accepted Du Bois's point of view in order to give black men as much support as possible.

Wartime mobilization disrupted college athletics, as some of the larger eastern schools such as Harvard and Yale discontinued varsity football for the season. Brown would play a full ten-game schedule, without, however, the services of its All-American. As a result of his off-the-field demands and a greatly inflated ego, Pollard had earned only slightly above a D average. He had failed several courses in four semesters, which dropped him below the minimum required at Brown for participation in intercollegiate athletics. Pollard's grades continued to fall, and by the spring semester of 1918 he decided to drop out of school and enter the military. He was appointed physical director of the army's Young Men's Christian Association unit at Camp Meade, Maryland.

The Maryland camp served as one of seven training facilities for the Negro 92nd Division, which were scattered around the country. Because of racial unrest and the army's reluctance to station black troops in the Deep South, the 92nd was not brought together until it reached France, and even then it never reached full strength. Pollard was not deployed with the 92nd; instead, he was reassigned as a physical director in the war department's new Student Army Training Corps program which was designed to train commissioned and noncommissioned officers on college campuses. Pollard was assigned to the SATC detachment at Lincoln University. Given the fact that his brother Leslie had been a football coach at Lincoln, there is reason to suspect that Pollard used his influence both within the army and in the black community to secure the appointment. In October, while the units of the 92nd and 93rd Negro Divisions fought against the German army on the Western Front, Pollard was transferred to the Lincoln University campus in Oxford, Pennsylvania, about forty miles southwest of Philadelphia. There he assumed his duties as athletic director of the Lincoln SATC unit, which included the position of head football coach.[13]

In the fall of 1918 Pollard moved to Philadelphia, where he enrolled as a part-time student at the University of Pennsylvania in the hope of rectifying his academic deficiencies and, after the war, entering the university's Dental School. Soon after the Armistice, the Lincoln SATC detachment was disbanded and Pollard, like many of his contemporaries, was quickly ushered out of the service. He retained his position as athletic director at Lincoln, which paid $50 a month, but soon realized that he needed to supplement that income in order to support his family. Pollard's first administrative decision was to solicit Paul Robeson to help with the coaching duties at Lincoln.

Paul Leroy Robeson had a background similar to Pollard's. Born on April 9, 1898 in Princeton, New Jersey, he attended racially mixed Sommerville High in Sommerville, New Jersey, where he played fullback on the football team. William Drew Robeson, Paul's father, had been born a slave in Martin County, North Carolina, on July 27, 1845. He escaped at age fifteen, joined the Union Army, and after the Civil War attended Lincoln University. Paul's thoughts of college centered on Lincoln because of his father, but he changed his mind when he scored the highest mark ever attained on the New Jersey High School Examination. He entered Rutgers University in the fall of 1915 on an academic scholarship.[14]

When freshman Robeson walked onto the practice field to try out for Rutgers football, the team had no blacks—indeed, like almost every other top-ranking college, Rutgers had never had a black player. In a day when football players typically lacked the mammoth height and girth they boast today (five members of the 1917 Rutgers team were five feet nine inches or shorter), Paul, at six feet two inches and 190 pounds, stood three to four inches taller and weighed some twenty pounds more than most others on the field.[15]

The "giant's" reputation had preceded him. Rutgers coach G. Foster Sanford had seen him play for Sommerville and had been duly impressed. The Rutgers first-stringers had also heard about Robey's athletic prowess—and skin color. Several of them set out to prevent him from making the team. On the first day of scrimmage, they piled on, leaving Robeson with a broken nose (an injury that would trouble him as a professional singer long after football), a sprained right shoulder, and assorted cuts and bruises. He was hardly able to limp off the field. Robeson had to stay in bed for ten days to allow his wounds to heal and thought of not returning to the football field. But his father had impressed upon him that "when I was out on a football field, or in a classroom, or anywhere else, I was not there just on my own. I was the representative of a lot of Negro boys who wanted to play football, and wanted to go to college, and, as their representative, I had to show I could take whatever was handed out. . . . Our father wouldn't like to think that our family had a quitter in it."[16]

After a visit and pep talk from brother Ben, Robeson went back out for another scrimmage. This time a varsity player brutally stomped on his hand. The bones held, but Robeson's temper did not. On the next play, as the first-string backfield came toward him, an enraged Robeson swept out his massive arms, brought down three men, grabbed the ball carrier, and raised him over his head—"I was going to smash him so hard to the ground that I'd break him right in two"—only to be stopped by Coach Sanford. Robeson was never again roughed up—not, that is, by his own teammates. Sanford then issued a statement that "Robey had made the team, and any player who tried to injure him would be dropped from it."[17]

Rutgers finished the 1915 season with a record of seven wins and one loss. By the 1917 season Robeson was the starting end on the Rutgers team that won seven, lost one, and tied one. After the 1918 season Walter Camp selected Paul Robeson as a first team All-American at end. Robeson became only the third black selected to Camp's first team, joining Pollard and Lewis, and the first black selected at end.

Robeson followed Pollard into professional football after graduating in 1919. That same year the Akron Indians signed Pollard to play professionally, largely because Akron had lost consecutive games to archrivals Massillon and Canton. In his first game, against Massillon before an estimated crowd of eighty-five hundred, Pollard quickly illustrated his worth, scoring the lone Indians touchdown in a 13-6 loss. Pollard was pleased with his first game in the informal Ohio League. He recalled that "for that game in 1919 I got $200.00 and my expenses. Later I said to myself, this isn't bad." But, as Pollard described it, he almost didn't play because of his inability to find housing:

> In 1919 a friend of mine approached me to play pro football in Akron, Ohio. I couldn't find a place to stay because of prejudice and almost didn't sign up. Anyway, I finally got an apartment and Paul Robeson joined me in 1920 at the end of the season. I was a halfback and Robeson was an end. Had a hard time at first, but then the team warmed up to me. We went through the 1920 season undefeated. We beat the Canton Bulldogs before 6,000 fans in Canton on Thanksgiving Day.[18]

The 1920 Akron Pros (the 1919 Indians folded and were replaced by a new organization in 1920) were literally led by Pollard, who co-coached the team from 1919 through 1921, making him the NFL's first black head coach. The long-standing controversy over when Pollard became the first black coach in the NFL is understandable because the position of professional head coach was very different then from what it is today. Pro teams placed less emphasis on who was head coach than did colleges. Coaches had a limited role and could not coach from the sidelines but had to sit in one place (on the bench). The captain really called the game, and if a substitute entered the game and talked to the quarterback, the referee was supposed to call a penalty. Pollard maintained that in conjunction with Clair Purdy, he introduced the more wide open system of play they had learned at Brown to the Akron team beginning in 1919. "From that point on," he insisted, "I was really the head coach. Even though the record books don't give me credit, I coached Akron in 1919, 1920, and in 1921." The Pollard-coached Pros of 1920 finished the season with eight wins, no losses, and three ties, and captured the first league championship.[19]

Pollard's salary while playing for Akron is one of the intriguing questions that may never be answered accurately. He claimed in a number of later interviews that he was paid $1,500 per game for important contests with Akron, which put him ahead of the $1,000 he said Jim Thorpe earned. The Professional Football Researchers Association estimates that the average pro salary for the era was $75 to $150 a game, with star players receiving a little more. The highest documented per-game salary for 1920 is the $300 that the Chicago Cardinals paid star quarterback Paddy Driscoll. George Halas, who paid the salaries of the Decatur Staleys in 1920, maintained that his players averaged $125 per game and that Guy Chamberlin got the biggest amount for the season, at $1,650. Thus it appears that Pollard exaggerated his per-game salary. Given his superior play for the Akron team, his contribution as coach, and his enormous appeal as a gate attraction, however, there is little reason to doubt that Pollard was one of the highest-paid players in the APFA in 1920.[20]

The earning potential in professional football along with his love for the game caused Robeson to join Pollard on the Pros in

1921. The Pros, with Pollard and Robeson on the 1920–21 teams, enjoyed an unbeaten streak of eighteen games. Robeson had an outstanding season playing both tackle and end, repeatedly breaking up plays coming around his side of the line. While Robeson got his opportunity to play because Pollard recruited him for the Pros, Pollard also aided Robeson in what would become his most famous profession. During the season, according to Pollard, he introduced Robeson to Florence Mills at the Café Zanzibar in the Winter Garden Theater in New York, where she offered Robeson an opportunity to sing during the floor show, thus launching his musical career.[21]

The new league continued to extend opportunities to black stars as its popularity grew. In 1922, Pollard helped organize, played for, and coached the new Milwaukee Badgers squad. Pollard was again joined by Robeson and another former black All-American at the University of Iowa, Fred "Duke" Slater, a six-foot four-inch tackle who divided the season between Milwaukee and Rock Island.[22] Pollard's roommate in college, Jay "Inky" Williams, a former Brown University end, was in his second season with Hammond as their left end, and was joined by John Shelbourne, a Dartmouth graduate. Shelbourne played fullback on the 1922 Hammond Pros for only one season. He ended his career by choice when he took a teaching position in a high school at Evansville, Indiana, in 1923.[23] Thus, in 1922 the NFL had at least five identifiable black players.

Although these few black players were given opportunities to play, they did not come without repercussions. Williams remembers that their relationships with white players were "very poor in some instances," while off the field the struggle against legal segregation was constant. While sitting in a hotel in Green Bay, Wisconsin, Williams and Pollard were "paged out of the dining room," then taken to the office and told, "We don't allow colored people to eat in our hotel." In Canton, Ohio, seated with some white players, Williams was allowed to go on eating—the management simply put a screen around the table.[24]

By the 1923 season, Robeson had departed football to pursue a theatrical career, and Shelbourne was teaching school. Pollard had moved on to Hammond as a playing coach. As Robeson and Shelbourne left the NFL three new black players entered the league. Edward "Sol" Butler, wingback/tailback from Dubuque, played for Rock Island, Hammond, and Akron in 1924 before finishing his career with Hammond and Canton in 1926. James Turner, a wingback from Northwestern, played his only season in the NFL for Milwaukee. And Dick Hudson, fullback who briefly attended Creighton, played with the Minnesota Marines. Hudson had been refused a tryout with Rock Island in 1923, before playing with Minnesota. He did not rejoin the team in 1924 but played with the Hammond Pros from 1925 through 1926.[25]

While no new black players joined the NFL in 1924, 1925 was a pivotal year for both the NFL and black players in large part because of the entrance of Harold "Red" Grange into professional football. On November 21, 1925 Grange wrapped up a brilliant collegiate career at the University of Illinois by leading the Illini to a 14-9 victory over Ohio State in front of ninety thousand fans in Columbus, Ohio. Earlier, the "galloping ghost" had set a college record by scoring six touchdowns in one game. The day after the Ohio State game, Grange sat on the bench and watched his new team, the Chicago Bears, beat Green Bay 21-0 at Wrigley Field. Four days later, on Thanksgiving day, Grange made his NFL debut in the Bears' scoreless tie against the Chicago Cardinals in front of thirty-six thousand fans at jam-packed Cubs Park.[26]

Grange was just what Bears owner George Halas and other NFL owners wanted, a bona fide white superstar who would attract fans. This is exactly what Grange did, and he was arguably one of the prime reasons for pro football's ascendancy to a major sport. Over the years Grange almost became bigger than the game itself. With Grange in their backfield, the Bears became the hottest ticket in pro football. After the regular 1925 season, they launched an eight-game barnstorming tour with Grange as the gate attraction, and when that was over, they played a nine-game tour that lasted into late January. Grange realized his potential to generate revenue, and hired C. C. "Cash and Carry" Pyle as his agent and manager. After their nine-game tour, Grange and Pyle split $100,000 in profits. After a week of rest, Grange and the Bears hit the road again. They wound their way through the South with three games in Florida and one in New Orleans before heading to the West Coast to play in Los Angeles, San Diego, San Francisco, Portland, and Seattle. When the second tour ended, Grange and Pyle split another $100,000.[27]

Because of Grange's barnstorming success, Pyle informed the Bears that Grange would not play for Chicago in 1926 unless Halas and his partner, Ed "Dutch" Sternaman, gave Grange one-third of the team. They refused, so Pyle decided he and Grange should start their own NFL franchise and place it in the media center of the world, New York City, to capitalize fully on the star's popularity. At the league's annual postseason meeting, Pyle proposed putting his team in Yankee Stadium, but Giants owner Tim Mara refused to allow it, claiming territorial infringement. When the league backed Mara, Pyle announced he was forming his own circuit—the American Football League—with his own team, the New York Yankees.[28]

Joey Sternaman, quarterback of the Bears and brother of club coowner Dutch, formed his own AFL team in Chicago and called it the Bulls. Sternaman then obtained a lease with Comiskey Park, sending the NFL Cardinals scurrying to smaller Normal Park. The other AFL teams formed were the Brooklyn Horsemen, Philadelphia Quakers, Newark Bears, Boston Bulldogs, and Cleveland Panthers; also added were the Rock Island Independents who jumped from the NFL to the new league. A ninth team, a traveling band without a home field but calling itself the Los Angeles Wildcats, also joined the league. Early in the 1926 season, the AFL looked as if it might offer serious competition to the NFL in attracting fans; but in reality the new league was a very risky endeavor. As Joey Sternaman recalled, "It was a big gamble and I got talked into making it. It seemed like a real good thing at the time. We actually had a pretty good team and we beat Red and his New York Yankees. But we didn't get the crowds and we just couldn't make it go."[29]

With a rainy autumn not helping its cause, the AFL stumbled from the start. By the end of October 1926, Newark and Cleveland had disbanded. In early November, the Brooklyn team shut down and merged with the NFL's Brooklyn Lions. Later that month, Rock Island, the only team with a known black player, Duke Slater, former tackle from Iowa, suspended operations. (Slater joined the Chicago Cardinals of the NFL for the remainder of the 1926 season.) With few teams left to play, the Yankees embarked on a tour of the South and West, trying to recapture the magic of Red Grange's 1925 tours. They weren't nearly as successful, and the AFL soon folded.[30]

As the short-lived AFL ended in 1926 so did the illustrious career of Fritz Pollard. He played his last game for Akron on October 10 against the archrival Canton Bulldogs. It was perhaps a fitting conclusion to Pollard's NFL career in that he faced his old rival, Jim Thorpe, one last time in gridiron combat. Akron and Canton battled to a scoreless tie. After the game, Frank Nied, the team treasurer, gave Pollard, who was thirty-two, his unconditional release as player and coach. An Akron news release stated that management took the action because Pollard "failed to play up to the form expected of him." Pollard was quoted in the article as saying that he had intended to retire after the season and wanted to end his professional career in an Akron uniform. He added that he had "never counted on being fired." Pollard made it clear that he would not sign with any other team and that he was heading home to Chicago.[31]

The release of Pollard after an eight-year career in the NFL was a sign of things to come for black players. The AFL's demise after the 1926 season created a large number of white players eager to enter, or reenter, the NFL. Apparently, in order to accommodate the extra white players from the AFL, the owners made room by dropping black players. Although the AFL failed, it illustrated Grange's appeal and professional football's growing popularity. However, very few black players were able to enjoy this newfound popularity. For, as the game became increasingly popular with Americans, black players were simultaneously eased off the field. From a high of five players in 1926, the NFL dropped to one in 1927–Duke Slater, of the Chicago Cardinals. In 1928 Harold Bradley, a guard with no college experience, joined Slater on the Cardinals, as the only two blacks in the NFL. Bradley played only one year and in 1929 Slater was again the lone black player in the NFL. In 1930 the Staten Island Stapletons played David Myers, a black New York University graduate, at left guard briefly. But again in 1931 Slater, in his last season with the Cardinals, was the only black athlete in professional football.[32]

By 1931 America was in the midst of the Great Depression. The number of unemployed Americans had climbed from 2 million in 1929 to 8 million by 1932. It was within this atmosphere of economic despair that Joe Lillard and Ray Kemp were evicted from the game, the last two black players to play in the NFL before a formal color barrier arose.

The 1932 season saw the emergence of the NFL's second black star, Joe Lillard of the Chicago Cardinals. Embraced by the black community and labeled the best player in pro football in 1933 by the black press, Lillard and Kemp were the last two black players to play in the NFL until 1946. Lillard's name is listed on the

Cardinals' roster for only two years, 1932 and 1933, but he left a large imprint on the NFL. As the only black NFL player in 1932, he was stigmatized as a disciplinary problem.[33]

Nicknamed "the Midnight Express," Lillard graduated from Mason City (Iowa) High School and attended the University of Oregon in 1930. Lillard emerged as Oregon's star in the backfield during the 1931 season. An extremely talented athlete, he posed a triple threat on the field—running, passing, and kicking. But just when Lillard seemed to establish himself as one of college football's stars he found himself out of the college game. On October 9, 1931, Jonathan Butler, commissioner of the Pacific Coast Conference, met with H. C. Howe, chairman of the Oregon Faculty Athletic Committee, Dr. Clarence W. Spears, Oregon's football coach, and Lillard. Howe had been investigating charges that Lillard had played semipro baseball with the Gilkerson Union Colored Giants of Chicago the previous summer. Lillard admitted that he had participated in a few games, but claimed that he had received money not as a player but as the team's chauffeur while driving the bus. Lillard claimed to have only filled in when an emergency arose. No immediate decision was made at this meeting but Chairman Howe indicated to Commissioner Butler that the investigation was still continuing.[34]

On October 11, 1931, Oregon beat the University of Washington, 13-0, at Seattle before thirty thousand fans. Lillard accounted for one touchdown when he scored on a rush from the one-yard line, and he intercepted two passes. The next game was scheduled against the University of Southern California, for Saturday, October 17. The Oregon team arrived at Glendale, California, on Friday, October 16. However, in Portland, Oregon, Commissioner Butler had submitted his resignation to the ten representatives of the Pacific Coast Conference, meeting in special sessions. The commissioner was upset that his efforts to have Lillard declared ineligible had been stymied by H. C. Howe, Oregon's faculty representative. Butler's resignation was rejected. On October 17, 1931, the *Los Angeles Times* reported that Joe Lillard had been declared ineligible to compete in varsity athletics for having played semipro baseball. Coach Spears said that Lillard was 50 percent of his offense and could see no reason for his suspension. The suspension of Lillard was felt immediately, as the University of Southern California overwhelmed Oregon 53-0.[35]

After being suspended, Lillard quit school to join various barnstorming All-Star pro football teams. On a clear, chilly Thanksgiving day on November 26, 1931, Lillard led the Bert Richey All-Stars to an 18-6 win over the Los Angeles All-Stars. Included in Lillard's exploits was a fifty-five yard touchdown run. Then on December 30, 1931, now with the Chicago All-Stars, Lillard helped defeat the Duffield Coast Stars, 20-6. Lillard's heroics in this game included a forty-five yard touchdown gallop. The stories of Lillard's feats were not confined to football circles on the West Coast—in fact, they had reached the powers-that-be of the National Football League.[36]

In 1932 Lillard was invited to join the Chicago Cardinals, replacing Duke Slater as the only black in the NFL during the 1932 season. The 195-pound, six-foot two-inch, triple-threat star made his NFL debut on Sunday, October 2, at right halfback. The Cardinals and the Portsmouth (Ohio) Spartans played to a 7-7 tie. Lillard's contribution was a drop kicked extra point.[37]

The next week, on October 9, the Cardinals faced the Chicago Bears, who ultimately won the league title. The *Chicago Daily Tribune* reported that Lillard was the Cardinals' best ball carrier and pulled the Cardinals out of bad field position in the last quarter with a fifty-yard punt from his one-yard line. The two teams played to a scoreless tie. The black *Chicago Defender*'s report on the game focused primarily on Lillard:

Lillard, Card halfback, gave fans plenty to rave over. This former Oregon star was the whole show and with his remarkable kicking and return of punts saved a show that was otherwise dull and devoid of bigtime class. . . . Lillard's name was left out of the early starting line-up, but he was in there when the gun sounded. . . . For weeks the papers had played up Grange, Nagurski, and Joesting, but all three flivered when compared with the Oregon flash.[38]

The next week, October 16, the *Boston Globe*'s headlines read:

NEGRO STAR OF CHICAGO ELEVEN THRILLS 18,000 BY
DAZZLING RUNS AS CARDINALS DOWN BOSTON

Lillard's contribution that day to his team's 9-0 win included a twenty-one yard run from scrimmage, a ten-yard completed pass, a ten-yard run from scrimmage, a drop kick extra point, a forty-four yard punt return, and a twenty-yard kick off return.[39]

On October 23, the Cardinals played a nonleague game against the Providence Steamrollers, members of the NFL from 1925 to 1931. The Cardinals won 7-0, with Lillard kicking the extra point and intercepting three forward passes on the Cardinals' goal line.[40] Just when it appeared that Lillard was coming into his own as a key player on the Cardinals' team, his playing time began to diminish, due apparently to growing friction between Lillard and Jack Chevigny, the Cardinals' coach.

On October 30, against the Brooklyn Dodgers, Coach Chevigny elected to play Lillard less than two minutes. The Cardinals won 27-7. In the next game against the Green Bay Packers on November 7, Lillard returned to the starting lineup, but the Cardinals lost 19-9. Lillard was in the starting lineup on November 13, against the Brooklyn Dodgers; however, the Cardinals lost their second game in a row 3-0. But more importantly for Lillard, the growing friction between Coach Chevigny and him came to a head. The game had been played in New York, and Lillard had been fined $50 for missing a "skull" practice the night before. In disfavor with Chevigny, Lillard was used sparingly in the Cardinals' next game, a 21-7 loss to the Staten Island Stapletons on November 20. After this loss, Lillard was suspended for the remainder of the season, which caused him to miss the last two games of the year against the Chicago Bears and Boston Braves.[41]

The *Chicago Defender*, reporting on Lillard's suspension from the Cardinals, speculated that there may have been other factors involved: "The suspension of Lillard by the Cardinals is traceable directly to the disfavor he ran into with his coach, Jack Chevigny, former ace at Notre Dame. They don't use Race boys up at Notre Dame, you know, and Chevigny may or may not have been prejudiced against the flashy black. The star is expected to be back in professional football next season however."[42] Lillard's suspension from the team in 1932 was apparently due to growing friction with teammates and management because of lackluster effort and a prideful attitude. Coach Chevigny explained that Lillard "disrupted practice by being tardy or absent, missed blocking assignments in games, and disobeyed team rules."[43]

Although these allegations may have been true, it seems strange Lillard was benched and eventually suspended just when he was emerging as a star on the team—especially since the Cardinals finished the season with a record of two wins, six losses, and two ties. Because Lillard played an instrumental role in wins against Boston and Providence and in the ties in Chicago and Portsmouth, and because little is known about Lillard and his experience with the Cardinals, several questions remain. For instance, how did his teammates treat him and did his on-the-field accomplishments cause jealousy? Did Coach Chevigny have some racial prejudice against Lillard? Did Lillard have a bad attitude that eventually required discipline? The answers to these questions may never be known, but it appears that Lillard was unfairly and gradually pushed off the Cardinals during the 1932 season.

The black press urged Lillard to be more accommodating, in that he had a great responsibility to other blacks to be successful. Al Monroe, sports writer for the *Defender*, urged Lillard to "learn to play upon the vanity" of whites. "He is the lone link in a place we are holding on to by a very weak string."[44]

After being suspended from pro football, Lillard did what made the most sense to him, which was to play pro basketball. On Friday, December 9, 1932, Lillard was in the lineup at guard for the all-black Savoy Big Five of Chicago. When the basketball season ended, Lillard joined black baseball's Chicago American Giants. He possessed an exceptional fast ball, but erratic control. He later switched to the outfield where his switch-hitting abilities could be used every day.[45] Lillard's ability to perform at the professional level in three sports leaves little question that he was a superior athlete. And after his suspension, he quickly reminded the Cardinals and the rest of the NFL that arguably he was one of the best players in the league.

In 1933 Lillard was reinstated by the Chicago Cardinals. In the first league game, the only two black players in major professional football opposed each other, Lillard of the Cards and Ray Kemp of the Pittsburgh Pirates. Kemp was a former tackle from Duquesne University. During his one year in pro football he had "an off-again on-again status." He was released after the third game, then recalled for the final three games of the 1933 season. The Pirates won the game 14-13, despite Lillard's contribution of passing for a sixty-yard touchdown.[46]

On October 8, the Lillard-led Cardinals beat the Cincinnati Reds 3-0 in what would be the team's only victory of the season. Lillard's seventeen-yard field goal was the margin of victory. Near the end of the game tempers flared. Lester Caywood, husky Cincinnati guard, landed a blow that sent Lillard to the turf. Lillard retaliated with a right uppercut to Lester's chin. Both players were ejected from the game.[47]

The next Sunday, October 15, Lillard scored all the Cardinals' points in a 12-9 loss to the Chicago Bears. This was probably the most significant game of the year, in that Lillard thoroughly embarrassed the great Red Grange. The *Defender*'s sports section headline read, "SORRY, RED; SEE YOU ON THE OTHER SIDE OF GOAL LINE" with a picture of Grange pursuing Lillard as he returned a Bears punt fifty-three yards for a touchdown. The black weekly described the run as "one of the prettiest ever seen in professional football." Grange "gave up hope of catching Lillard and quit running. Grange was the safety man, but Lillard sidestepped the 'Sorrel Top' just as he had done six other would be tacklers before scoring a touchdown."[48]

Although Lillard was enjoying individual success, the Cardinals as a team were not. On November 20, the Brooklyn Dodgers beat them 3-0, and handed the Cardinals their eighth defeat in nine games. Lillard was not in the starting lineup. On Thanksgiving day, November 30, the Chicago Bears beat the Cardinals 22-6. For the second straight game Lillard did not start. He did get in the game against the Bears long enough to score the Cardinals' only touchdown with a five-yard burst of speed around left end.[49] Again Lillard's playing time was reduced, just as it had been late in the 1932 season. Yet Lillard led the team in scoring, accounting for nineteen points, which consisted of rushing for a touchdown, passing for a touchdown, a punt return for a touchdown, and a PAT. The next closest Cardinal in scoring accounted for only twelve points. The Cardinals as a team only scored fifty-two points the entire season! Although the Cardinals were a terrible team, Lillard arguably was their most valuable player.

In the season finale on December 3, the Cardinals battled the Boston Redskins to a scoreless tie. Lillard did not start, but was soon in, running the offense for injured quarterback Roy Lamb. When the 1933 NFL season drew to a close there would be major changes in store for pro football in general, and black players specifically. Lillard's season came to an end against the Boston Redskins, but so too did participation by black athletes in the entire structure of the National Football League.[50]

From 1934 until 1946 no blacks were allowed to play in the NFL. NFL owners may have used Lillard's volatile personality as an excuse to ban other black athletes. Proud and hot-tempered, Lillard rarely overlooked a racial slur or dirty play. When wronged he retaliated, thereby earning a reputation for being a "bad actor."[51] Unlike many of the early black players who seemingly were thankful for the opportunity to participate in professional football, Lillard was neither humble nor accommodating.

Ray Kemp of the Pittsburgh Pirates and Joe Lillard were the last blacks to play during the 1933 season. After being released in 1933, Kemp began a long career as a college football coach. He felt that racism was the sole reason for his release, saying, "it was my understanding, that there was a gentleman's agreement [among the owners] in the league that there would be no more blacks."[52] NFL owners, like their baseball counterparts, denied the existence of a racial ban. "For myself and for most of the owners," Art Rooney of the Pittsburgh Steelers explained decades later, "I can say there never was any racial bias." George Halas of the Chicago Bears declared in 1970 that there had been no unwritten exclusionary agreement "in no way, shape, or form." Tex Schramm of the Los Angeles Rams did not recall a gentlemen's agreement. "You just didn't do it [sign blacks]—it wasn't the thing that was done."[53]

Schramm's admission reveals how prevalent racist attitudes were, so strong that no written or overt agreement was required. Jim Crow was simply the national order of things. In 1935 Coach Paul Schlissler, who replaced Chevigny in 1933, conceded as much when he noted that Lillard had been a victim of racism:

He was a fine fellow, not as rugged as most in the pro game, but very clever. But he was a marked man, and I don't mean that just the southern boys took it out on him either; after a while whole teams, Northern and Southern alike, would give Joe the works, and I'd have to take him out." Lillard's presence, the coach continued, made the Cardinals a "marked team" and the "rest of the league took it out on us! We had to let him go, for our own sake, and for his, too![54]

Although not as controversial as the first black heavyweight champion Jack Johnson, in many ways Lillard was just as non-compromising. His accomplishments on the field generated publicity especially in the black press. Perhaps his tremendous athletic ability threatened white players, coaches, and owners. Surely NFL owners did not want the reputation of soliciting black players while major league baseball was all-white.

During the 1920s, Fritz Pollard has observed, the fledgling NFL teams may have signed black All-Americans to gain recognition and fan support. Having gained popularity and stability during the 1930s, the league was no longer willing to sign "name" black players. Pollard in particular felt that George Halas "used" him to get the Bears recognition: "He used me to get recognized, then Halas refused to play Akron in 1923 unless Akron dropped me. And he refused to play Milwaukee the next year when I went up there." Pollard complained bitterly in a 1976 interview that "George Halas used me to get every goddam thing he could. Then after he used me and got power, he raised the prejudice barrier. If George Halas was still like he was then, he wouldn't have allowed a black player in Chicago because he was prejudiced as hell." When confronted with Pollard's charges in the mid-1970s, Halas refuted them all: "He's a liar. At no time did the color of skin matter. All I cared about was the color of blood. If you had red blood, I was for you." When asked why there were no blacks in the NFL from 1934 until after World War II, Halas replied, lamely, that he did not know: "Probably the game didn't have the appeal to black players at the time."[55]

While there is no clear-cut evidence of a formalized racial barrier, no black players participated in the NFL after it was reorganized following the 1933 season. The league reorganization took place under the leadership of George Preston Marshall, creating two divisions and a championship game. It has been speculated that the Boston Redskins' owner may have included an unwritten recommendation for the exclusion of black players as part of his reorganization plan for the league submitted at the owners' 1933 meetings in February and July. Scholar Gerald R. Gems suggests that George Halas, "whose influence in league matters was always substantial, may have provided the necessary support. . . . He probably respected Marshall's business acumen, and in a quest for respectability among the working class, perceived it as a sound business decision along with the other changes proposed by Marshall to increase fans' interest."[56]

After the 1933 season NFL owners obviously initiated a policy of barring blacks from the game, but why then? There are several possible reasons. First, during the owners' meetings in February and July Marshall probably advocated a ban. It became clear that he had no love for black players when he became the very last NFL owner to integrate his team after the color ban was lifted in 1946. Second, with attendance down team owner Dr. David Jones sold the Chicago Cardinals in midseason to Charles Bidwell, who remained at the head of the organization until his death in 1947. Bidwell promptly brought in new front office personnel and a new head coach in Schlissler, who later stated that Lillard's presence caused other teams to try and injure him, thus forcing the Cardinals to release him for his own protection. Perhaps as a new owner, Bidwell was more than willing to go along with Marshall, Halas, Rooney, and the other owners in banning blacks. And finally, the Depression hurt all areas of American life, sports included. Pro football, less established in the country's heart than the college game or professional baseball, suffered more than either of these longtime favorites. The NFL had been shrinking since the start of the Depression, hitting a low of eight teams in 1932. Although league membership grew to ten teams in 1933, and remained relatively stable through the rest of the 1930s, compensating black players in this dismal economic environment probably didn't make good business sense to white team owners.

The increasing acceptance of professional football by fans during the 1920s allowed owners to release African American players who had earlier been needed as drawing cards. There was not enough support in the black community for professional football to justify black player participation. Black players also created logistical problems. Lodging was a problem, along with service in restaurants, during this Jim Crow era. The color ban, which lasted for twelve seasons in the NFL, in effect made black players invisible to every NFL team.

3. Invisible Men

The NFL Color Barrier

The exploits of Negro league baseball players and teams prior to the integration of major league baseball have been well chronicled. Players such as Satchel Paige, Josh Gibson, and Cool Papa Bell, along with teams such as the Pittsburgh Crawfords, Homestead Grays, and Birmingham Black Barons are legendary in African American sport history. But just as these black baseball players and teams were virtually "invisible" in the eyes of major league baseball, so too were black football players and teams in the eyes of the NFL during its color barrier. However, while black baseball was a major part of black society, black football was not. Thus, black football players and teams enjoyed much less popularity and are not viewed as historic icons, as are their baseball counterparts. Though this can be explained again by baseball's place among black Americans, it was also because baseball's color barrier was in place much longer—from the end of the nineteenth century until 1947. The NFL's color barrier only lasted twelve seasons, which prevented the formal organization of teams and leagues as in baseball.

The creation of the color barrier in the NFL appears to have happened informally, in that there is no written documentation between owners. Instead there seems to have been a gentlemen's agreement among owners not to sign black players to team contracts. According to the African American press, the owners expected to make big money with the new divisional realignment implemented in 1934, and "in the midst of the Depression it was considered unseemly for a black man to earn more money than a white man, whatever the field of operation." Although the charges may have had some substance, it appears that any gentlemen's agreement was very informal in 1934, yet may have become more standardized later in the decade. It is known, for example, that Ray Kemp was offered a contract by Pittsburgh in 1934, but turned it down so that he could complete his college education. George Halas, moreover, wanted to sign black halfbacks Ozzie Simmons in 1936 and Kenny Washington in 1939, but apparently could not get the consent of fellow owners. In 1934–35, few black sportswriters focused on the apparent problem in the NFL for fear of bringing attention to a color barrier, which might or might not exist, and perhaps worsen the situation.[1]

George Preston Marshall was likely the driving force behind the color ban. The West Virginia-born owner, one of the most influential in the league, had gained prominence by bringing organization and structure to the NFL. During the 1920s the league was a bit helter-skelter with franchises often going out of business or relocating. In 1933, at Marshall's request, the league was reorganized into two five-team divisions with a season-ending championship game. Four years later, Marshall established a franchise in the South by transferring his Boston Redskins' team to Washington, D.C., a segregated city. To avoid offending Marshall, southern white players, and fans, NFL owners may have tacitly agreed to shun black athletes. Marshall himself once publicly vowed that he would never employ minority athletes, declaring that his team was "the team of the South." That clearly did not include southern blacks. Entering the southern market, Marshall hoped that football would soon rival all-white major league baseball in popularity. Millions of dollars were to be made; historically when vast sums of money are involved, blacks are either placed at the end of the line or, as in this case, taken off the line altogether.[2]

Some owners, like George Halas, lamely attributed the absence of blacks in the NFL to the lack of quality players. Others, like Art Rooney, claimed that financial constraints prohibited NFL teams from developing adequate scouting systems. Financial realities no doubt discouraged owners from scouting black colleges, but there were several standout black athletes on major white college teams in the 1930s who too were overlooked. Since white players were scouted and signed, it seems reasonable to expect that black athletes, who played in the same conferences, would have been discovered. But none were, until 1946.[3]

Black professional football players, just like black baseball players, formed their own teams that played each other as well as some white and integrated semipro teams. With virtually no coverage from the white press and limited coverage by the black press, details about many of these teams are sketchy. Beginning in 1928, Fritz Pollard organized an all-star black professional football team on Chicago's South Side with the expressed intent of showing that interracial football could be played without ugly incidents. The team, which became known as the Chicago Black Hawks the following season, scheduled games against white professional and semiprofessional teams in the Chicago area. Pollard's South Side eleven were composed of aspiring young players as well as former NFL veterans Ink Williams, Sol Butler, and Pollard himself. Duke Slater also played for the team during the 1928 campaign when he was not otherwise engaged with the Chicago Cardinals. While Pollard proved his point that teams with both black and white players could compete without serious incident, the South Side team drew poorly at the gate. Consequently Pollard and his general manager, Albert C. Johnson, took the Black Hawks on the road during the fall and winter months for the next three seasons. Most of the games the Black Hawks played were against white all-star teams in California. With the Depression worsening, however, the team was forced to disband in California during the 1931–32 season because of poor attendance. Many of the players, nearly broke, were stranded on the West Coast.[4]

One of the first black teams to appear after the establishment of the NFL color barrier were the Chattanooga Ramblers. They were formed during the 1934 season by "Big Bill" Grossman, a prominent white sportsman of Chattanooga and the sole owner of the all-black team. The Ramblers played other all-black teams such as the Black Vols of Knoxville, Tennessee, and the Purple Pirates of Nashville. The Ramblers issued an open invitation, offering to play any team that wanted a game. They had a relatively brief life, and by the late 1930s the team apparently had disbanded.[5] This scenario was a common one for many black professional football teams during the 1930s, largely because of low attendance. However, for Pollard the risk of losing money and possible failure were outweighed by a more important goal. By creating a competitive black professional team Pollard hoped to persuade NFL owners to lift their color barrier. If NFL owners would consent to playing his black team, this might facilitate the signing of black players again by various NFL teams.

Late in the summer of 1935, Pollard initiated his plan by accepting an offer to coach a professional, all-black Harlem football team organized and managed by Herschel "Rip" Day, an athletic promoter and Lincoln University alumnus. The team was named the Brown Bombers in honor of rising heavyweight boxing contender Joe Louis. Day was determined to make the Brown Bombers the finest black pro team in the nation, on par with Bob Douglas's famed New York Renaissance Big Five basketball team.

Pollard was attracted to the offer to coach the Brown Bombers at least in part by his concern about the failure of NFL owners to sign black players for a second consecutive season. As he had earlier attempted in Chicago with the Black Hawks, Pollard tried to showcase the best available black football talent and demonstrate once again that blacks and whites could compete on the gridiron without serious incident. He was determined to schedule exhibition games with the local NFL teams—the Brooklyn Dodgers and the New York Giants—to underscore his point. During the season, Lewis Dial of the *New York Age* printed a rumor, probably started by Pollard, that the Giants had challenged the Bombers to a game in late November. Dial quoted Pollard as saying that if the November date was not acceptable, "a post season game will be arranged."[6] In fact, neither of New York's NFL teams were interested in playing the Brown Bombers or any other black team. Pollard's negotiations with Giants owner Tim Mara may have been outright unfriendly, for he later held Mara along with Halas as being primarily responsible for the color ban in the NFL.

Despite Pollard's continuing and ultimately unsuccessful efforts to schedule a game with either the Dodgers or Giants, he and Day were pleased with their success in putting together a first-rate professional team. Pollard brought in former Chicago Cardinal halfback Joe Lillard as the centerpiece of the Bomber backfield and signed Dave Meyers who had played for two seasons with the NFL Dodgers. He also added halfback and former Morgan College star Thomas "Tank" Conrad to help provide a potent offense. Scheduling only white professional teams from the Northeast and playing their games at Dyckman Oval across the river from Harlem in the Bronx, the Bombers got off to a fast start. After five games they were undefeated, racking up ninety-two points to their opponents' nine.[7]

Although the city's black newspapers gave the Bombers ample coverage and duly praised Pollard and his players, the team struggled financially. Average attendance at Dyckman Oval was about fifteen hundred per game, barely enough to cover players' salaries. To create more excitement and help boost attendance, Pollard instituted a number of trick plays and unorthodox formations, including one called the "aeroplane shift" that the *Amsterdam News* claimed baffled opponents. Midway through the season, Pollard reluctantly agreed to allow the team to sing spirituals and "truck" from the huddle to the line of scrimmage. He told a reporter that at first he had opposed the singing and dancing routine, which the team sometimes used in practice drills, but "then it struck me all of a sudden that it might help them, and it might aid in selling the team to the public." Truckin' and singing became trademarks of the Brown Bombers, but Pollard stopped short of clowning antics, long a part of African American professional sports and most recently popularized by the black Cincinnati Clowns in baseball. The Bombers' showmanship was popular with the Harlem fans and did increase attendance, but Pollard admitted near the end of the season that "we've lost about $5,000 so far." He added, however, that "we're getting new capital in next year and some new players and I'm sure we'll be a big financial success."[8]

In 1936 Pollard's Brown Bombers were not the only black professional football team. The Chicago American Giants, founded by H. G. Hall, owner of the black Chicago American Giants baseball team, and W. A. Bacharach Smith began play that same year. Hall's experience as the owner of a black pro baseball team had taught him the importance of talent, and he quickly began to recruit the best collegiate players in the country. For the first time many black players from black colleges and universities were given an opportunity to display their talents. On October 11, the Giants debuted by defeating the Evanston Wolverines 19-0. Jack Hart, former player for Wilberforce, was the quarterback; Nile Andrews, Texas college star, fullback; Shag Jones, All-American from Morris Brown, right halfback; and Jock Thornton, also of Morris Brown, at right end. All the players demonstrated skills refined during their collegiate years.[9]

The Brown Bombers of 1936 achieved some major victories that established them as the best black pro team of the decade. On October 30 they trounced the Newark Bears 41-0, before three thousand spectators. In the game played on November 6, the Brown Bombers scored in every period, to defeat the Yonkers Tigers 33-0. In the final game of the season, played on November 13, the Bombers tied the Providence Steam Rollers, 0-0. They dominated the opposition, recording six wins, no defeats, and one tie. Considering the rout of the Newark Bears and a 29-0 whitewash of the still highly regarded Frankford Yellowjackets, Pollard felt he could legitimately claim that a number of black players were capable of playing in the NFL. Yet, as before, NFL owners showed no interest in either scheduling or recruiting players from the Brown Bombers.[10]

In 1937 the Brown Bombers continued their on-the-field success. They opened the season with a 7-7 tie with the Brooklyn Eagles on October 3. Three days later the Bombers received their first loss of the season against the Danbury Trojans, 0-12. They rebounded on October 22 against the White Plains Bears. A crowd of five thousand witnessed Joe Lillard make a drop kick from thirty-five yards out, giving the Bombers a 3-0 win. A week later, in a 13-6 victory over the Connecticut Yankees, the Bombers demonstrated that they were not a one-man team as Charles Paige, a former Hampton Institute ace, led them to victory. He did not score any points, but his punt returns and kicking kept Connecticut at a disadvantage. The Bombers ended their season with wins over the Brooklyn Tornadoes on October 31, 25-0; the Jersey City Giants, 28-0, on November 12; a loss on November 26, 0-17 to the City Islanders; and on December 3 in Nashville, Tennessee, before a crowd of over four thousand, the Bombers defeated the Silver Streaks 13-7. In all, the Bombers finished the 1937 season with five wins, two losses, and a tie.[11]

Before the opening of the 1938 Brown Bomber training camp at Verplanck, New York, *Amsterdam News* sports columnist J. Wayne Burrell announced that James Semler, manager of the Black Yankees Negro National League baseball team, was organizing a "big time" black professional football team by the same name. In an interview with Burrell, Semler conspicuously failed to mention the Brown Bombers. The Black Yankees' manager remarked that "with the exception of one or two players appearing with white professional elevens, there is no place on the 'big time' for our stars of color." Semler said he was "appealing to the magnates in the two Negro (baseball) leagues and other sports minded business men to cooperate with [him] in trying to create a place in the Sun for these Negro gridiron heroes." The implication of Semler's remarks was clear: He was challenging Pollard's team for supremacy among New York's black fans and obviously did not consider the Brown Bombers a legitimate force in providing exposure for black players.[12]

Semler's remarks must have hurt Pollard, who had organized and coached black all-star teams since the late 1920s and whose Bombers were clearly the outstanding black team in the country. What was worse, it soon became apparent that Semler had made a deal with Cuban-born Alessandro "Alex" Pompez, owner of the Negro National League's Cuban Giants baseball team and a convicted numbers racketeer, to gain exclusive use of Dyckman Oval, which Pompez owned. When Pollard learned that the Bombers would not be allowed to use Dyckman Oval for their home games and realized that no suitable stadium close to Harlem was available, he promptly resigned as coach. He simply stated to the press that he was "no longer connected with the Brown Bombers football team nor any other in any capacity." The Brown

Bombers struggled on for several more years as a road team, but could not continue to pay the best black players and never recaptured their past glory. Just before the wartime mobilization the franchise folded.[13]

However, before they disbanded, the Brown Bombers joined the integrated Northwest Football League in 1938. The NWFL, a league of semipro teams, had existed since 1936, and in 1937 it included two black players: Bobby Vandever of the champion Des Moines team and Don Simmons of the Cedar Rapids Crushers. Unfortunately, the NWFL was on its last legs in 1938, and coverage was spotty. Nevertheless, the Brown Bombers were the first all-black team to play in an integrated professional football league.[14]

Although the Brown Bombers were the most visible black team during the NFL's color ban, several other black teams created opportunities for black players. The Chicago Comets began play in 1939 after being founded by Kenneth Campbell, an Illinois vehicle tax inspector, and W. A. Donaldson, a Chicago bail bondsman. Coached by Don Simmons, Duke Slater, and Henry Hatcher, the Comets began the season by winning their first three games, in the process defeating the all-white Macomb (Illinois) Eagles 10-0, then the Midwest semipro champions.[15] The Comets disappeared after 1939, only to reemerge the next year as the all-black Chicago Panthers. Media coverage of black pro teams was very limited, and primarily confined to the black press. And with black baseball and black college football receiving the bulk of black papers' sports stories, black pro football was not covered on any consistent basis. Still, teams continued to be created and in 1946 an all-black football league was formed, the Virginia Negro League. The VNL included teams in Richmond, Norfolk, Portsmouth, and Newport News. The league lasted only one season, but all four teams played as independents for several years thereafter. Besides playing each other, they played games against local black colleges like Virginia Union and Norfolk State.[16]

Many all-black teams created during the twelve-year ban were successful not only in terms of wins and losses, but more importantly by providing blacks the opportunity to play. As the founder of black professional football, Fritz Pollard's principal motive after retirement was to pressure NFL owners into signing top-quality black players. The case of the University of Iowa halfback Ozzie Simmons may have convinced Pollard that no matter how good a black player might be, he stood no chance of breaking into the NFL.

A four-sport high school star from Fort Worth, Texas, Ozzie Simmons was a 185-pound running back at the University of Iowa, where he played beginning in 1934, along with his brother Don and two other blacks, Windy Wallace and Homer Harris. At the end of his junior year in 1935, Simmons was named to the Associated Press All-American second team, scoring five touchdowns on runs each of over fifty yards. However, Simmons did not make the American Coaches Association All-American team, and was never selected during any of his three superb seasons. The presence of University of Illinois coach Bob Zuppke on the board of five coaches who picked the "official" All-America team may have been a factor in Simmons's failure to be selected. (Fritz Pollard contended that his son, Fritz Jr., who wanted to play at Illinois after dropping out of Brown, was told that Zuppke did not allow blacks on the Illinois team.) Rumors, which had begun in 1934, contended that Simmons was prevented from making first-team All-American because his teammates resented the attention he was getting and refused to block for him. He was the logical choice for team captain in 1936, but his teammates voted instead to do away with the honorary position for that year.[17]

Simmons's final collegiate season in 1936 was somewhat disappointing. In mid-November, after a 52-0 loss to Minnesota,

Simmons left the team after being berated by Coach Solem for a lack of effort. Simmons was reinstated for the final game and scored a seventy-two-yard touchdown to help Iowa defeat Temple University. Despite considerable talent, he was bypassed for both the team's most valuable player award and for All-American honors. Rather, Homer Harris, a black end, was voted the team's most valuable player at the end of the season. Harris was also selected captain for 1937, becoming the first black player to captain a Big Ten football team. The selection of Harris by Iowa's white players may have indicated that his personality was more acceptable to them than Simmons's. Although he had a rocky last season Simmons still hoped to land in the NFL. In late 1936 Simmons told reporters that he hoped to make $5,000 the following season as a pro and remarked that he had "one or two offers to play in the NFL in 1937. I understand Negroes may be barred," he added, "and I may not get a contract but I hope I do." Simmons failed to get an NFL contract that year or any other. He signed with the Patterson Panthers the following season, a semi-pro team of the American Professional Football Association, where he played a number of years.[18]

Ozzie Simmons was but one of the many outstanding black players who played major college football, especially in the Big Ten Conference. Others included Horace Bell and Dwight Reed of Minnesota, Clarence Hinton and Bernie Jefferson of Northwestern, and Willis Ward of Michigan, all talented athletes bypassed by the NFL because of their skin color. (Jefferson, a gifted running back, was eventually signed by the Chicago Rockets in 1947, long after his prime.)[19] By the late 1930s it was painfully clear that the color barrier would continue to be rigidly enforced. However, in 1938 a ray of hope appeared in the form of an interracial football game.

About the same time that Pollard resigned as coach of the Brown Bombers, black sportswriters were encouraged by the announcement that George Halas had agreed to play a charity exhibition game pitting his Bears against a hastily assembled black all-star team in Chicago. The game was scheduled to be played on September 23, 1938 at Soldiers' Field. Proceeds from the game were to go to Hull House, the Abraham Lincoln Center, and the Central District of the United Charities. With a crowd of forty-five thousand expected to see this historic contest, many African Americans believed this game was a perfect opportunity to showcase black players' skills and demonstrate that black athletes could compete in the NFL. The black All-Stars were coached by former black NFL players Duke Slater and Ray Kemp, selected by popular vote, and made up of players who had already graduated. Many of the players selected were from black colleges. The backfield consisted of "Big Bertha" Edwards of Kentucky State, "Tank" Conrad of Morgan State, Ozzie Simmons, and Joe Lillard. However, unlike the backfield, the line was light and inexperienced. Moreover, the team had less than two weeks to practice.[20]

The game was a rout, with the powerful Bears winning 51-0. The All-Stars made only four first downs and lost fifty-one yards rushing. The Bears, forced to punt only once, amassed 605 total yards. "We've just finished witnessing the most disappointing sports spectacle of the decade . . . a 'promotion' which will set Negro college football back years," lamented William G. Nunn of the *Pittsburgh Courier*.[21] "I'm not offering any alibis," Ray Kemp explained after the game. "We lost to a great team . . . one of the greatest in pro football, but I do regret that we didn't have a longer period to train. Several of my best men didn't arrive until less than a week before the game."[22]

An unconfirmed story leaked out during the game that the Bears' defense had hinted to Kemp that they might get together and "allow" an All-Star to score at the beginning of the second half. But this turned out to be just a rumor.[23] The All-Stars did win a small battle, in that three Bears were put out of the game, including Lou Gordon who suffered a fractured knee after being tackled by Don Simmons. Reportedly all the All-Stars were able at least to stand on their feet at the end of the contest.[24]

The game was not well attended. In fact, of the expected forty-five thousand, only six thousand attended. Many correctly believed that the All-Stars didn't have much of a chance against the Bears, and that they had not been together long enough. The morale of the All-Stars before the game did not help their performance either. It was understood that each player would receive his round trip expenses to and from the city or town from which he was called, plus $100 for playing in the game. The afternoon of the game, word had reached them that they might not get their money after the game, because the squad was larger than the projected thirty men. However, before the game they were assured by Coach Kemp that they would all receive their money Friday night after the game, which they ultimately did.[25]

After the charity game against the Bears, several black players were able to sign on with white semiprofessional teams in various leagues. In 1939 Joe Lillard signed on with the Union City Rams, a New Jersey team in the APFA. Lillard now joined Ozzie Simmons, who played in 1938 for the Patterson New Jersey Sox, also of the APFA. The APFA teams were white semipro teams that were used as a kind of minor league for the NFL. Simmons may well have been the first black to play in this league. Lillard was elected team captain of the Rams, making him the first black player to be captain of a major football team. Lillard took a slap at the NFL and their level of competition during an interview on October 6, 1939. When asked whether the APFA teams were as tough as the National Football League's, Lillard noted: "They don't play as classy a brand of football of course because the star [white] players are generally found in the majors but they play a hard . . . game that is certainly just as tough. I don't think I have even been hit as hard by a major leaguer as I was struck by three members of a Jersey semi-pro team."[26]

The 1939 season ended with Lillard and Simmons demonstrating that they were two of the best players in the APFA. However, Lillard was traded from the Rams to the Brooklyn Eagles, where he went on to give some outstanding individual passing performances. Simmons led the APFA in scoring, and was viewed as the primary reason why Patterson was the champion of the league.[27] Although Simmons and Lillard were successful standouts in the APFA, neither were offered NFL tryouts in 1940. While Lillard and Simmons were shut out of the NFL in 1940 after stellar seasons in the APFA, the previous year America had witnessed the emergence of the greatest college player since Red Grange. Kenny Washington, UCLA's phenomenal black halfback, was one of the greatest college football players of all time. On December 4, 1937, before eighty thousand fans at the Los Angeles Coliseum, Washington completed the longest in-air pass documented in the history of American football—seventy-two yards. No one, not even in the NFL, had thrown a pass that far.[28]

Kenny Washington was raised in Los Angeles by his grandmother. Kenny's father, Edgar Washington, also known as "Blue," passed only his athletic ability on to his son. Blue was an outstanding baseball player, playing professionally with both the Kansas City Monarchs and Andrew Rube Foster's Chicago American Giants. Blue also had a few parts in various movies, including *Gone with the Wind*. Between baseball and the movies, Blue was virtually never home and spent little time with his son. So Washington referred to Blue's brother Rocky as his father. Rocky was a lieutenant, the only black officer of any rank in the Los Angeles Police Department. It was Rocky who helped Kenny develop the athletic skills that enabled him to excel while at UCLA.[29]

At UCLA Washington played with two other outstanding black athletes—Woody Strode and Jackie Robinson. Washington and Strode played together from 1937 through 1939; they were joined by Robinson for one year in 1939. During UCLA's undefeated season of 1939 Washington played left halfback, Robinson right halfback, and Strode end. Although Washington finished the 1939 season leading all college players in total yardage with 1,370, he was named only to the All-American second team.[30] (Two white players, Tom Harmon, right halfback from Michigan and Grenville Lansdell, Washington's counterpart at left halfback for USC, both finished second behind Washington in total yardage, yet were named to the first team.) After the All-American selections were made, *Liberty* magazine polled more than sixteen hundred college players to see who they thought should be an All-American. The magazine then chose the eleven players. Only one player of the 664 nominated received the vote of every player who opposed him—Kenny Washington. Washington was the only unanimous choice of his peers, and as a result he was awarded the Douglas Fairbanks Trophy as the nation's outstanding player.[31]

Like Washington, Strode grew up in Los Angeles. Strode met Washington when he was seventeen, and they became lifelong friends. Strode was a 220-pound end with speed and sure hands. Strode recalled how he didn't back down to name-calling at UCLA: "Some players would insult me. They'd call me a nigger and I'd fight over that. I got kicked out of a few ball games based on that name-calling. . . . If they hit Kenny, if they called me a nigger, then they were going to sleep. We had white kids on our team that would react to nigger just like I did. We got so beat up, but it was like a badge of honor."[32] At the end of the 1939 season, Washington and Strode would have made excellent additions to any NFL team. But once again the implicit policy of barring blacks, no matter how talented, was unyieldingly enforced by all NFL owners.

At least one white sportscaster was outraged by this injustice. In an "open letter" over the airwaves NBC broadcaster Sam Balter asked NFL owners why "nobody chose the leading collegiate ground gainer of the 1939 season." NFL scouts, he continued, all ranked Washington the best player in the nation but "none of you chose him." Balter expressed bitter disappointment "on behalf of the millions of American sport fans who believe in fair play and equal opportunity." He concluded by offering airtime to owners to explain why neither Washington nor Brud Holland, who played end at Cornell and was named to several All-American teams, were "good enough to play ball on your teams." The offer was not accepted.[33]

Although Washington was not drafted, there still appeared to be a window of opportunity for him to play in the NFL. He was invited to play with a team of college all-stars against the NFL champion Green Bay Packers. Designed to generate fan appeal in 1934, the preseason game was played annually for charity between the defending NFL championship team and a collection of college all-stars. If Washington produced an outstanding performance, it might cause some owner to break the gentlemen's agreement and sign the best college football player in America. On August 29, 1940, at Soldiers' Field in Chicago, Washington played with the college All-Stars who lost to the Packers 45 to 28, in front of eighty-four thousand spectators, including over ten thousand black fans. Many blacks came to the game just to get a glimpse of the "Kingfish," as Washington had come to be affectionately known. Washington scored a touchdown and thrilled the crowd with dazzling runs and passes.[34]

Interestingly, sportswriters differed over whether Washington's performance was strong enough to justify participation in the NFL. Jimmy Powers, a white columnist for the *New York Daily News*, urged Tim Mara and Dan Topping, owners of the New York teams, to sign the UCLA star. "He played on the same field with boys who are going to be scattered through the league," Powers noted, "And he played against the champion Packers. There wasn't a bit of trouble anywhere."[35] But Fay Young, a black writer for the *Chicago Defender*, felt that Washington's performance on the field was not strong enough to warrant his joining the NFL. "As a defensive man, Washington wasn't so hot. . . . On defense, he wasn't in there to nail the Green Bay ball carriers. . . . Washington wasn't any Joe Lillard or Fritz Pollard. Washington's play didn't stamp him of the caliber of all-round player whom we expected to see—and far from the caliber which is demanded by the professional football clubs."[36]

After playing in the All-Star game and before returning to Los Angeles, Washington played one game with the all-black Chicago Panthers. The Panthers defeated the Waukegan Collegians on September 11, by a score of 42-0. The Panthers were coached by Duke Slater, and also had Ozzie and Don Simmons on the roster. The Waukegan team only had twelve players.[37] Its manager blamed the short roster on the booking agent, Abe Saperstein. Apparently Saperstein had booked a game the previous year against the Brown Bombers and paid players with a check that bounced, causing many of the players to refuse to continue to play for the team. Saperstein, a shrewd businessman, later founded the Harlem Globetrotters.

Washington had stayed around Chicago after the College All-Star Game at the request of Bears owner George Halas. While waiting to hear from Halas Washington played with the Panthers. Washington remembered that after waiting a week Halas told him that "he couldn't use me." Apparently Halas had consulted several NFL owners concerning the signing of Washington and had been denied.[38]

Although barred from the NFL, Washington simply had too much talent to be ignored. Promoter Larry Sunbrock realized that Washington could draw fans and scheduled two special exhibition football games in 1940. The games pitted a college all-star team featuring Washington against two semipro teams in the LA Coliseum. Washington received $1,000 per game and his former teammate Strode $750 per game. Washington was clearly the main attraction, as the team was billed "The Kenny Washington All-Stars." The two semipro teams were members of the Pacific Coast League started by Paul Schlissler, former head coach of UCLA, the NFL's Chicago Cardinals, and the Brooklyn Dodgers. Although as coach of the Cardinals, which subsequently initiated the color barrier in the NFL, Schlissler released Joe Lillard, he later signed Washington and Strode to play in the PCL. Originally there were five teams in the league: San Diego, Fresno, Salinas, Hollywood, and Los Angeles. In relative terms the money paid to Washington and Strode was astronomical in that players in the semipro leagues generally received $35 a game. Most players in the semipro leagues and in the NFL had full-time jobs to help supplement their incomes. After Washington graduated he joined the Los Angeles Police Department with the help of his uncle, Rocky. After graduation Strode worked for the District Attorney's office as an escort for prisoners.[39]

Race had an impact on the field and off for Woody Strode, especially in relation to his personal life. In 1940 Strode, a black man with Native American ancestry, married Princess Luana Kalaeloa of Hawaii. (Princess Luana was related to Queen Lilly Ukulani, former monarch of Hawaii.) As an employee of the LA District Attorney, Burron Fitts, who was up for reelection, the media exploited Strode's interracial marriage as a political issue. Fitts lost his bid for reelection, and Strode lost his job. However, Schissler, owner of the Hollywood Bears, asked Strode and Washington to join his team. Strode earned $100 a game, plus a percentage of the gate, as an end for the Bears. Don Hutson, by comparison, was receiving about $175 a week as an end with the Green Bay Packers in the NFL. The Bears played at Gilmore Stadium, which, when filled to capacity, enabled Strode to make $300. Washington received $200 a game, plus a percentage of the gate, allowing him to take home $500 some weeks. Ironically, just as the NFL didn't want Washington and Strode, they were not begging to be let in either. According to Strode, he and Washington "were making more money than the guys in the NFL. Right on the tickets it was printed, 'The Hollywood Bears with Kenny Washington vs. . . .' That's the kind of marquee value Kenny had. . . . Schlissler was shrewd, he would pay Kenny so much, and he would pay Rocky so much. That way the players didn't think Kenny was getting that much more than them. . . . Kenny and I were in paradise."[40] Because of the money they were being paid, Washington and Strode experienced no financial hardship by being excluded from the NFL. But just when the criticism of NFL owners for not drafting Washington had all but ceased, Jackie Robinson became eligible for the NFL draft.

In 1939, during his first year at UCLA, Robinson played alongside Washington and Strode at right halfback. Robinson grew up in Pasadena, a suburb of Los Angeles, and he attended Pasadena Junior College for two years before enrolling in UCLA. A tremendously gifted athlete, Robinson was described by Strode as:

> the best all-around athlete UCLA has ever had. . . . He was well-coordinated, he had great speed, a lot of strength, and he was very quick. Jackie became the only man in UCLA history to letter in four varsity sports: track, baseball, basketball, and football. He was the national long jump champion in 1940, and he was the basketball team's highest scorer the two years he played. Baseball was his weakest game, but in football he

excelled. In 1939 he led the nation in average yards per carry, a little over 12 yards per run from the line of scrimmage.[41]

Strode remembers Robinson as somewhat withdrawn, a loner with a fiery personality and a volatile temper. One of the biggest misconceptions about Robinson was that he possessed a natural ability to subdue anger. At a time when many blacks accepted societal inequalities, Robinson did not. An incident that took place right before Robinson arrived at UCLA illustrates his innate rage toward the racially intolerant. After playing a softball game, Robinson was giving his friend Ray Bartlett a ride home, Bartlett was riding on the running board. En route they passed a white motorist who started calling them "niggers." When they eventually got to a traffic signal, Bartlett reached out and slapped the man across the face with his baseball glove. Frightened, the man realized that he had made a mistake and attempted to flee. But Robinson was not ready to let it end there. He chased the man down and forced him off the road. Bartlett attempted to cool Robinson off but he wouldn't back down, he was in a rage and "ready to kick the guy's ass." However, before a physical confrontation ensued the police arrived and promptly arrested Robinson.[42]

Robinson left UCLA before graduating because of financial difficulties and a desire to support his mother. He was clearly one of the best—if not *the* best—running back eligible for the NFL draft. But once again it was made clear that the color barrier was in full effect. Despite the fact that he led the nation in average yards per carry, Robinson was not drafted by any NFL team. However, like Washington before him, he played in the annual All-Star game. The 1941 All-Star game once again pitted the best college players against the NFL champion Chicago Bears. On August 28, before 98,203 fans at Soldiers' Field in Chicago, the Bears defeated the college All-Stars, 37-13. Robinson thrilled the large crowd with exciting runs, and scored the last touchdown for the All-Stars with a thirty-nine-yard catch and run. Robinson quickly won his teammates over and they made sure he was protected against dirty play. Once when the Bears were roughing him up, no fewer than a dozen All-Stars started onto the field, but the officials quickly made them return. After the game Dick Plasman, Bear end, declared, "That Jackie Robinson is the fastest man I've ever seen in uniform. I thought Don Hutson was fast, but he could spot Don five yards and pass him by. The only time I was worried about the game was when Robinson was in there."[43]

After Robinson's performance, Fay Young, who had criticized Washington's performance a year earlier, began to address some larger issues:

> The game ought to make the United States Army and Navy wake up. Every time a Negro who is qualified asks to join a particular branch of either service, there is a cry that Negroes and whites can't do this or that together. A great example of what can be done is shown in this college All Star vs. pro game for charity. Men from all sections of the country were on the Bears' team. Since professional football draws the color line when it comes to players, no Negro was with the Bears. But the Bears played against Robinson and marveled at his ability. The Green Bay team played against Kenny Washington in 1940 and the New York Giants played against Bernie Jefferson of Northwestern and Horace Bell of Minnesota in 1939.
>
> What the pros need to do is look at that 50,000 crowd which watched the East vs. West all star (Negro League All-Stars) baseball game at Comiskey park in July. Maybe the Cardinals or Bears could use an additional 10,000 each time they play here. One thing is certain, 10,000 times whatever the admission price, is nothing to be sneezed at.[44]

Although NFL owners did not heed Young's advice to bring on black players to attract black fans, the NFL and America were on the verge of a dramatic transformation. America's participation in World War II was instrumental in bringing drastic change to the NFL. The 1941 season was the last played before the wartime draft would require NFL teams to reorganize. For African Americans, America's immense mobilization effort meant a window of opportunity might be opened. Black labor leader A. Philip Randolph was determined to see this happen as he organized an all-black march on Washington to protest the government's discriminatory hiring practices in the war industries. That proposed action prompted FDR to issue Executive Order 8802, creating the President's Committee on Fair Employment Practices. With the bombing of Pearl Harbor on December 7 and America's subsequent involvement in World War II, the wartime emergency sharply increased black employment. The war labor shortage facilitated the migration of millions of blacks from the rural South to the urban North.

Black attitudes about America changed as a result of the war and important events occurred both at home and abroad which eventually triggered a mass protest against segregation and discrimination. Even before Europe drifted toward war, African Americans were keenly aware of the contradictions involved in America's opposition to the master race ideology of Nazi Germany and the suffocating caste system a majority of blacks faced in the supposedly democratic United States.

The war forever changed the face of professional football. More than six hundred NFL players, coaches, and officials participated in the conflict. Twenty-one of those men never came home, including twelve active players. Attendance at NFL games dropped as the war preoccupied the country. Suddenly football didn't matter. In 1942, total paid attendance dropped to 887,920, the lowest since 1936. Roster limits were lowered from thirty-three to twenty-eight players and a free substitution rule was adopted.[45] Many older players who had retired were called back into the league. Rather than give blacks an opportunity to play, NFL owners employed retired white players. George Halas, for instance, coaxed Bronko Nagurski out of retirement in 1943 to join the Bears. Nagurski was thirty-four and hadn't played in five seasons, but he helped fill a war-depleted Bears roster.

Several service football teams were organized during the war to keep up morale. The March Field Fliers were one such service team organized by Paul Schissler. The prime purpose of the team was to provide some entertainment and make money. The team played for Army Emergency Relief, a charity for the families of soldiers killed or injured. Schissler told his players with the Bears that if any of them were drafted by the military they should contact him, and he would place them on the team as opposed to entering active military service. Strode and Washington were both drafted and Schlisser had them placed on his team. Strode played but Washington could not because of a knee injury. Still, Schissler was able to assemble some of the greatest black and white players in football because of the war. The Fliers played other service teams, semipro teams, and had games against some of the colleges and universities. The Fliers were very successful in that they won most of their games, but at the end of the 1944 season the team was disbanded along with many other service teams for the final push in the war effort.[46]

Although Washington wasn't able to play on the Fliers because of a knee operation, the government still used him. During the war Washington was sent overseas on the USO tour to talk to segregated black units. Washington was one of several black athletes asked to participate on these tours. "The idea behind these USO tours was to keep the black soldiers quiet by promising them things would get better after the war. Just keep working within the system and things will change."[47] Washington's message was reinforced by the most popular black athlete in America, heavy-weight champion Joe Louis. Louis traveled well over seventy thousand miles during World War II on various USO tours.

For blacks the war was a hypocritical conflict between racist Nazis and racist Americans. Nevertheless blacks once again illus-trated their loyalty and patriotism in the face of racial prejudice. Segregation was the rule in the army as in many areas of Ameri-can life. And it was segregation that brought Joe Louis and Jackie Robinson together as privates in an all-black cavalry unit sta-tioned at Fort Riley, Kansas. However, Lewis's experience in the military was vastly different from Robinson's. Prior to enlisting, Robinson had played football during the 1941 season with the Los Angeles Bulldogs of Schlisser's PCL, but left the team after he got a better offer to play semipro football in Honolulu. In fact Robinson was on a ship returning to California when the Japan-ese attacked Pearl Harbor. He returned home, was drafted, and ended up at Fort Riley, where he played on the football and base-ball teams. He was then transferred to Camp Hood in Texas, where he was involved in an incident that would again be a testa-ment to his strong, fiery, noncompromising personality. Though the story is false (other than his being exonerated of court-mar-tial charges) it has been told in various versions, which only adds to the legend surrounding him.[48]

According to Truman Gibson, another soldier at Camp Swift and later a Chicago attorney:

> Jackie went to Camp Swift and was getting on the bus going back to camp when the bus driver, who along with most of the white bus drivers in the South was deputized and carried a pis-tol and whose firm resolve was to see that Negro soldiers would get to the back of the bus, said, "All right, nigger, get to the back of the bus."
>
> Jackie said, "I'm getting to the back of the bus. Take it easy."

"You can't talk to me like that."

Jackie said, "Well, I can talk to anybody any way I want."

So he [the bus driver] pulled his pistol, and Jackie said,

"That's a fatal mistake." He says, "You're going to eat that son of a bitch." So Jackie took it and broke every tooth in the guy's mouth, and they discharged Jackie for the good of the service. That's the Jackie Robinson story.[49]

During the war years several outstanding black players at white universities emerged as legitimate pro prospects. However, they were all bypassed even though the NFL was in desperate need of players. Bill Willis, born in Columbus, Ohio, on October 5, 1921, entered Ohio State University in 1941 and graduated four years later. As a 212-pound tackle nicknamed the "Cat" for his quickness, Willis played three varsity seasons. Ohio State won conference titles in 1942 and 1944. As a senior Willis was regarded as one of the greatest tackles in football, and was named to several All-American and all-star teams. Understanding that there was a color barrier in the NFL, Willis felt that his football career was effectively over. After he graduated in 1945, he took a football coaching position at Kentucky State.[50]

Marion Motley was another black player whose talents could have aided any NFL team. Born in Leesburg, Georgia, on June 5, 1920, Motley played football at McKinley High School after his family had migrated to Canton, Ohio. In the 1930s McKinley's archrival was Massillon (Ohio) High School, coached by Paul Brown. The McKinley teams with Motley could never beat Brown's Massillon teams, but Motley's performances made a lasting impression on Brown. Brown left Massillon in 1941 to coach Ohio State through the 1943 season, where his star player was Bill Willis. After high school Motley worked in the steel mills for two years before he entered the University of Nevada, where he starred for the Wolfpack from 1941 to 1943. During the war

Motley was drafted by the navy and played for the Great Lakes Naval Training team, which was coached by Brown in 1944 and 1945. After being discharged from the navy, Motley received no offers from any NFL team.[51]

Although Claude "Buddy" Young was perhaps the most sensational college gridiron star during the war years, he too was initially excluded from the NFL. As a freshman running back at the University of Illinois in 1944, he captured national attention with his exciting runs. A native of Chicago, the five foot five inch "Bronze Bullet" possessed exceptional quickness and acceleration. A track star, he won the national collegiate championships in the hundred- and two-hundred-yard dashes, tied the world record for the forty-five- and sixty-yard dashes, and was the Amateur Athletic Union's hundred-meter champion. Young was drafted by the navy in late January 1945. Initially he reported to the Great Lakes Naval Training Station, but he was eventually transferred to the naval base at Fleet City, California, where he played on the local service team. The Fleet City Bluejackets were one of the best teams on the West Coast. They completed the season undefeated, and beat the El Toro California Marines in the championship game 45-28. In that game Young returned a kickoff for a ninety-four-yard touchdown, a kickoff eighty-eight yards for a touchdown, and took a handoff thirty yards for a touchdown. The Bluejackets then challenged the unbeaten West Point team, but the cadets refused the invitation. Young's performance won accolades from players, coaches, writers, and fans. Rumors circulated that once Young had fulfilled his service obligation he would be drafted by the NFL. But the color line held firm. Since he was not drafted, Young returned to the University of Illinois, where in 1947 he helped the Illini win the Rose Bowl.[52]

For Willis, Motley, Young, and many other black players, as the war drew to a close the winds of change began to blow. In 1944 the seeds that would change the face of professional football and baseball were planted. Frustrated in their attempts to break into the NFL, a group of wartime power brokers met in a hotel room in St. Louis on June 4, 1944, and discussed the possibility of forming their own pro football league. Arch Ward, the sports editor of the *Chicago Tribune* who had organized the Chicago College All-Star Game and baseball's all-star game, chaired the meeting, which included representatives from Buffalo, Chicago, Cleveland, Los Angeles, New York, and San Francisco. By the end of that day, the group had laid the foundation for a proposed league and chosen its name: the All-American Football Conference.[53]

During that same year plans for another football league were made. Red Grange, president of the United States Football League, announced that "our new league has set up no barriers. Any athlete, regardless of color, will be invited to try out for our teams, and if he has the ability, he will be welcomed. The Negro boys are fighting for our country; they certainly are entitled to play in our professional leagues."[54] However, the USFL never played a single game.

For African Americans the desegregation of major league baseball was more important than pro football during the 1930s and 1940s. The national pastime was extremely popular among black athletes and dozens of highly qualified blacks played in the Negro Leagues. Unlike in football, however, blacks had never participated in major league baseball in the twentieth century. Indeed, during the early 1930s when the NFL was desegregated, black writers condemned baseball for being the "only national sport that bars black players."[55] On November 25, 1944, Judge Kenesaw Mountain Landis, commissioner of baseball since 1919, died. He had staunchly opposed the participation of black players in major league baseball, and his death brought a glimmer of hope that now baseball's racial policy could be challenged.

In 1945, rumors began to spread about the possibility of a black athlete breaking the color barrier in baseball. These rumors circulated primarily around the activities of Branch Rickey, general manager of the Brooklyn Dodgers. Rickey had started his own team in the Negro Leagues, and called them the Brown Dodgers. The team was Rickey's way of scouting black ballplayers. He realized that a number of black players had the necessary talent to play major league baseball. It was hard to ignore the exploits of Satchel Paige and Josh Gibson, especially when he ran a team that had been nicknamed the "Bums" because of their ineptness on the field. The Brooklyn Dodgers were perennial losers of the National League's pennant, and Rickey had been brought over from the St. Louis Cardinals to turn the team around.

On October 23, 1945 history was made when the Brooklyn Dodgers signed Jackie Robinson to a minor league contract with the Montreal Royals. He was given a $3,500 signing bonus and received $600 a month to play for Montreal. Robinson played the entire 1946 season with the Royals, batting .349, and stealing forty bases, with a league-leading .985 fielding percentage at second base. He highlighted his first year by batting .333 in the Little World Series as Montreal beat Louisville, four games to one.[56] The 1946 season quite simply belonged to Jackie Robinson. African Americans now anxiously anticipated Robinson being given the opportunity to play for the Dodgers in 1947. But while much of the media attention was focused on Robinson and baseball, his signing began a chain reaction that forever changed the face of professional sports.

Black football players wanted to know whether pro football would follow the lead of baseball and reintegrate as well. In early 1945 the newly formed AAFC looked as if it too would erect a racial barrier like the NFL's. In fact, the new league made several attempts to merge its newly formed teams into the NFL. In a final effort Jack Keeshin, who owned the Chicago Rockets franchise, and Paul Brown, head coach of the Cleveland Browns, met with NFL Commissioner Elmer Layden in April. They argued that a merger was the only way to prevent costly bidding wars. Layden rejected their overture. By the winter of 1945–46, the AAFC had designated the fall of 1946 as its inaugural season.[57]

The AAFC, which had only existed on paper until 1946, drafted Steve Juzwick, Harry Hopp, Frankie Albert, Elroy "Crazy-legs" Hirsh, and several other college stars who had played on service teams. Black players, however, were initially ignored. Buddy Young was bypassed, perhaps because he still had college eligibility. But to the dismay of many blacks, the AAFC also over-looked Kenny Washington and Woody Strode.[58]

Hopes for desegregation were stalled when the Miami Sea-hawks entered the league in January 1946. Wendell Smith wrote that Miami was the most "nazified of all the cities in the world on matters of racial equality." Like their NFL rivals, AAFC officials denied the existence of a color barrier. But Smith argued that blacks would be excluded. Smith felt that blacks had hopes that the AAFC would be "operated by more liberal men—men who wouldn't draw the color line as the NFL has been doing for years. But it's the same old story. Negroes won't be permitted to play."[59]

Ironically, the pessimism expressed by Smith and other black sportswriters that the AAFC would not include blacks changed to optimism that the color barrier would be lifted in the NFL. The primary reason for this was that by 1946 the Cleveland Rams had moved their franchise to Los Angeles. Twenty-seven days after winning their first NFL championship in 1945, the new Los An-geles Rams became the first major pro sports team to take up res-idence on the West Coast. Since he had purchased the team in 1941, owner Dan Reeves had dreamed of plugging into the lu-crative Pacific market. Estimating that airplane travel was finally feasible, he shocked the Cleveland patrons by going West. Reeves came from a wealthy family that owned a chain of grocery stores in New York, which Reeves sold for millions. He became an investment banker and started his own company. But he loved football, which prompted him to buy the Rams. The Rams were managed by Charles Walsh, better known as "Chili." His brother Adam was the head coach of the team.

The Rams and the newly formed Los Angeles Dons of the AAFC hoped to use the 103,000 capacity Municipal Stadium, which was publicly owned, as their home.[60] At a Coliseum Commission meeting held in late January 1946 with representatives from the Rams and Dons, several black writers, including Halley Harding of the *Los Angeles Tribune* and Herman Hill, the West Coast correspondent of the *Pittsburgh Courier*, objected to use of the coliseum by any organization that practiced racial discrimination. During this meeting Harding delivered a dramatic speech for integration. He traced the early beginnings of pro football in America, pointing out that Fritz Pollard, Paul Robeson, Sol Butler, Duke Slater, and other black athletes had played prominent roles in the league's success, only to be barred in later years. He ascribed the Jim Crow policy directly to the influence of George Preston Marshall, owner of the Washington Redskins. He charged that since Joe Lillard had played for the Chicago Cardinals in 1933, no black had been given a chance to play in the NFL. He pointed to the exploits of Kenny Washington and wondered why he had never been signed by any team in the NFL. Harding reminded the members at the meeting of the sacrifices and ambitions of World War II veterans.[61] "Chili" Walsh pledged that he would sign Buddy Young after he graduated, and that "Kenny Washington or any other qualified Negro football player is invited by me at this moment to try out for the Los Angeles Rams." Representatives from the Rams and the Dons promptly announced their intent to sign black athletes and the Coliseum Commission allowed both teams to use the stadium.

The promise to bring on black players caused a lot of speculation as to who would be signed and when, or whether the Rams and Dons had made a pledge that they had no intention of living up to. At a meeting in early February with representatives of the black press, Walsh answered questions surrounding the possible signing of Kenny Washington, Woody Strode, and Charles Anderson, standouts of the Hollywood Bears Professional Football League champions. When Walsh indicated that he would not sign the trio while they were under contract with any other team (all three had signed one-year contracts which were in effect until August), W. R. "Bill" Schroedar, general manager of the Hollywood Bears, indicated that the team would not stand in the way of their advancement.[62]

And so the twelve-year racial ban established in the National Football League appeared ready to be lifted. This color barrier had been erected because of several key factors: after the unstable early years of the 1920s in which many black players were allowed to participate as drawing cards, by the early 1930s the NFL was gaining in popularity and had established itself as a major professional sport; the white owners themselves were the driving force behind the color barrier. Although there is no written evidence of a "gentlemen's agreement" between the owners, clearly there was unity between all NFL owners to keep black players out of the league. And finally, George Preston Marshall, who had great influence on other owners in the league, probably initiated the ban. At his request the NFL was reorganized into two five-team divisions with a season-ending championship game. Marshall himself once publicly stated that he would never hire black players, and NFL owners may have agreed to keep black players out to appease Marshall.

4. Reintegration

Washington, Strode, Willis, and Motley

When World War II ended, many African Americans were skeptical about the lasting impact of progress made as a result of the global conflict. World War I had raised black hopes and expectations only to see them dashed by a powerful postwar surge of white racism. To be sure, black Americans had been more cautious in extending their full support to the war effort in the second conflict and were more assertive in demanding fair treatment at home and overseas. The threatened March on Washington in 1941 and race riots in Detroit, Harlem, and other cities during 1943 clearly suggested a definite restiveness among African Americans.

In athletics, dramatic breakthroughs leading to the integration of the major professional sports closely followed the Japanese surrender at Tokyo Bay in 1945. Branch Rickey's signing of Jackie Robinson to play for the Brooklyn Dodgers' Montreal farm team in 1945 was clearly the most heralded and symbolically important of these. The fledgling National Basketball Association (which grew, in part, out of the Basketball Association of America), the NFL, and its rival All-America Football Conference also integrated in the immediate postwar years. Many blacks who regarded advancement in sports as a benchmark of progress saw these events as portending a brighter future.[1]

On March 21, 1946 the Los Angeles Rams signed Kenny Washington to play football in the NFL, paving the way for Washington to become the first African American to play in the NFL since Joe Lillard and Ray Kemp in 1933. The twelve-season ban of black players in the NFL had finally been lifted. "Chili" Walsh, general manager of the Rams, made the announcement at the Alexandria Hotel in downtown Los Angeles. Walsh informed the press that Washington's contract had been purchased from Coach Paul J. Schissler of the Hollywood Bears. Walsh and the Rams declined to announce the terms of the contract. Washington's uncle, Rocky, handled the negotiations; he had a no-cut clause added that ensured Washington would be paid for one year even if the Rams only used him for publicity purposes. Walsh assured Rocky that they were genuinely interested in Washington not only as a drawing card but because of his ability. It was a good thing that Rocky insisted on the no-cut clause, as Rams backfield Coach Bob Snyder later conceded that the team had only signed the twenty-seven-year old black star as a precondition to obtaining the Coliseum lease. He also believed that Washington would attract black fans and boost gate receipts. "I doubt we would have been interested in Washington if we had stayed in Cleveland," Snyder observed.[2]

Washington's appearance in a Rams uniform was scheduled for the last week of August 1946, against the integrated College All-Stars at Soldiers' Field in Chicago. Walsh praised Washington for his athletic abilities, and also addressed the obvious issue of race: "I have heard many fine things about Washington, both as a player and a man, and I feel certain that he will be a credit to our ball club and to his race. . . . I look for other teams in the league to accept him in good grace just as he has always been given fair treatment and won the respect of all who have played with and against him in intercollegiate football and in his professional play on the coast during the past five seasons."[3] While praising Washington's past athletic accomplishments on various integrated teams, Walsh failed to mention that Washington had not received an opportunity to play in the NFL after graduating in 1939. There was no question that Washington was a much better player in 1939 than by 1946. However, the opportunity for black players to now play in a league that had barred them for twelve seasons became the immediate focus for many as opposed to the injustice inflicted by the color barrier.

Although the Rams were commended for breaking the NFL color barrier, Washington was no longer in his prime because of age and injuries. Having already undergone two knee operations, Washington would need a third before the season began. The Rams could have signed a younger and healthier black player if they were exclusively concerned about talent. Nonetheless, the black press hailed the signing of Washington. "Kenny finally gets a break," wrote Wendell Smith in the *Pittsburgh Courier*. Parallels were drawn with Jackie Robinson. "Both athletes had performed brilliantly at UCLA. Both were pioneers for their race."[4] However, Washington's experience in professional football was vastly different from that of Robinson in baseball. Robinson was given a legitimate opportunity to contribute to the success of his team, while Washington was not. Signed for political reasons which essentially boiled down to the use of the LA Coliseum by the Rams, Washington suffered physically and mentally during his brief professional career. Ironically, the same politics that helped create an opportunity for Washington also created a chance to play for his best friend and former teammate.

In mid-May, the Rams purchased Woody Strode's contract from the Hollywood Bears. In his autobiography Strode describes how he came to be a member of the Rams:

When Kenny signed, they had to get him a roommate. He could have gotten along with the white boys on the team, Bob

Waterfield and Jim Hardy and all of those boys from UCLA and USC. But the thinking then was that he had to have a running mate, another black person to live with on the road. They asked him to select somebody. Kenny told them he wanted me. They spoke of my marriage to a Hawaiian. They tried to use my marriage to keep me off the team. But Kenny had power at that point and he said, "I want my buddy." That's how I came to play for the Los Angeles Rams.[5]

Kenny Washington, Woody Strode, and Jackie Robinson became the three blacks most responsible for integrating pro sports in postwar America. Yet both Washington and Strode played for the Rams a full year before Robinson reached the major leagues.

To obtain its lease from the Coliseum Commission, the Los Angeles Dons of the AAFC had also agreed to give blacks the opportunity to play. But the Dons violated their pledge, and did not sign a black player during their inaugural season. The Dons were sharply criticized by the black press, but did not bring on blacks until 1947. Meanwhile, AAFC Commissioner James Crowley reminded fans that the league had "no rule that bars a Negro athlete from playing." The AAFC, he informed a black newspaper, "is just what the name implies; it is All America in every respect." However, the only other team to prove that point in 1946 was the Cleveland Browns.[6]

On August 2, Paul Brown, coach and part-owner of the Browns, invited former Ohio State All-American tackle Bill Willis to training camp at Bowling Green University. Willis had been the head football coach at Kentucky State College during the 1945 season. After one year of coaching Willis realized he still wanted to play, so he took a leave of absence from his coaching duties. Brown had coached Willis at Ohio State and was fully aware of his athletic capabilities. The invitation to training camp caught Willis by surprise. Because of the black ban it was "inconceivable to me that I would play pro ball." Feeling that the door to the AAFC was closed to blacks and barely open in the NFL, Willis had agreed to join the Montreal Alouettes of the Canadian Football League. However, Brown was able to convince Willis to stop at Bowling Green, Ohio, where the Browns were training, on his way to Canada and to try out for the team. While in camp Willis quickly won the admiration of his teammates. Brown, well aware of Willis' abilities, signed him to a contract, and had him participate in the team's first intersquad scrimmage: "Bill, who had the quickest defensive charge after the ball was snapped of any defensive lineman I ever saw, lined up right on Mo Scarry's head, and every time Mo tried to center the ball, Bill was on him so quickly that Mo couldn't even make the exchange with our quarterbacks."[7]

Called the "cat" because of his tremendous speed off the ball, Willis proved right away that he would be a major asset to the Browns. After a couple of days it was obvious that Willis had to be added to the team, so the Browns duplicated the policy of the Rams and sought a black roommate for him to prevent social friction. On August 17 Marion Motley arrived at the Browns' training camp. Motley too had played under Paul Brown in 1945 at the Great Lakes Naval Training Center, where he starred as the team's fullback. Following his navy discharge Motley had returned to his Canton home with no interest in returning to the University of Nevada and resuming his college career. He was nearly twenty-seven years old and, with a family to support, had taken a mill job. Like Willis, Motley was invited by Brown to try out. Once at the Browns' training camp Motley ran the fastest times in the sprints and left little doubt that he too had the ability to play professional football.[8]

Paul Brown claimed that his primary concern in signing Willis and Motley was winning football games: "I never considered football players black or white, nor did I keep or cut a player just because of his color. . . . I didn't care about a man's color or his ancestry; I just wanted to win football games with the best possible people."[9] Brown was well aware of the impact that the signing of Jackie Robinson had made in 1945. Yet Brown argued that "I had made up my mind long before Rickey's action that I wanted both Willis and Motley to play for us." Well aware of the attention that breaking football's color barrier would receive, and in order to soften the publicity, Brown waited until the team was in training camp before asking both players to join. However, his decision was not entirely supported. A few owners, Brown recalled, took exception to his actions.[10] In fact, possibly more than a few owners disagreed with Brown, for the Browns were the only team in the AAFC to play black players during its inaugural season.

For Willis and Motley the opportunity to play professional football caused an immediate financial change in their lives. Motley's steel mill salary was approximately $65 per week or about $3,300 for twelve months. Willis made $2,800 annually as head football coach at Kentucky State.[11] Motley's contract called for him to be paid $4,000 and he received a $100 signing bonus. Willis too signed a $4,000 contract with a $100 signing bonus. Willis and Motley were now both making more money while having to play for only about five months, and they could work in the offseason to supplement their incomes. In comparison with other players on the team, Willis and Motley's salaries were fairly equal. Otto Graham, Jr., who played quarterback, had the highest salary on the 1946 Browns. Graham received $250 per month by the Browns while he fulfilled his naval duties. Once discharged, he was paid $7,500 with a $1,000 signing bonus. Louis R. Groza, who place-kicked and played tackle, was given $300 per month while in the armed forces and paid a $5,000 salary after being discharged. Dante Lavelli (end) and Frank Gatski (center) in 1946 both received $3,500 salaries with $500 signing bonuses.[12]

Now that Washington and Strode of the Rams and Willis and Motley of the Browns had reintegrated professional football, questions remained as to what impact they would have on their individual teams. Before moving to Los Angeles in 1946, the Cleveland Rams had finished the 1945 season with a record of 9 and 1, and had defeated the Washington Redskins in the championship game. The Rams' championship team had no shortage of good backfield men, and the question became how would they utilize Washington's abilities. Coach Adam Walsh said, "We'll use him where we can get the most good out of his many outstanding abilities. There is always one thing that any player can do better than anything else and we will use Kenny where his assets as a passer and runner will give us the strongest possible four-man combination on the field at one time."[13] In other words, Walsh didn't really know how he was going to use Washington.

When the season started for the Rams, neither Washington nor Strode saw much playing time. In the annual preseason game between the NFL champion and various college All-Stars, played on August 31 in Chicago, the Rams lost to the College All-Stars 16-0. After the team's return to Los Angeles, Coach Walsh announced that there would be changes made in the starting lineup, and that both Washington and Strode would see plenty of action the following week. However, Walsh did not have a lot of pressure on him to play Washington since he had undergone two knee operations in the spring. Washington did get his knees in good enough condition to play, but that was all. He never regained the cutting ability and lateral movement he had once possessed. On the other hand, Strode was never really given a chance to play. The Rams management disapproved of his marriage to a Hawaiian, and if they could have chosen another black player they would have. But Washington was adamant about wanting his friend, so Strode spent much of the year sitting on the bench, collecting $350 per week.

Both Washington and Strode experienced racial prejudice while in the NFL. Most incidents occurred off the field while they were traveling with the team. Strode recalled that "sometimes the team would stay at the Hilton and Kenny and I would have to go find somewhere else to stay. If we were lucky, we'd stay with a friend or relative."[14] In fact, when the Rams played their first game of the season against the Chicago Bears in Chicago, Washington and Strode were not allowed to room with the team at the Stevens Hotel. When Strode was told of the situation by Washington, he asked where they were going to stay. Washington informed him that "they're going to give us $100 apiece to go find some place else to stay." Since this was a healthy sum, Strode quipped, "Well, what the hell, let's be segregated!"[15] Washington and Strode moved into the Persian Hotel, the most luxurious black hotel in Chicago, where they were able to hear Count Basie's band play that night in the club section of the hotel. The Rams quarterback Bob Waterfield went to check on Strode and Washington later that night, to inform them that arrangements had been made for them to join the team in the Stevens Hotel. However, Strode and Washington were happy where they were: "Forget that, boy," replied Strode, "I'm going to be segregated, spend this hundred dollars, stay right here, and listen to the Count play his music."[16] Recognizing the irony of segregation, Waterfield ordered himself a drink and socialized with his two teammates until the wee hours of the morning.

Strode and Washington's visibility generated a tremendous amount of pride and admiration in blacks across America. Washington and Strode did not realize this until they began traveling with the team:

Traveling with the Rams made a big impact; we discovered how popular we were across the country. The black kids outside California used to tell Kenny and me how much they enjoyed listening to our games on the radio while we were still playing at UCLA. Until that time, we didn't realize what a unique thing we had done.[17]

Neither Washington nor Strode recalled many racial incidents on the field. Both felt that while on the football field everyone was trying to hurt everybody, and that it was difficult to know who was trying to hurt you simply because you were black. Strode recalled only one incident where Washington was lying on the ground and an opposing player attempted to kick him in the head. Luckily Washington was quick enough to move out of the way. However, Washington and Strode spent most of their time sitting on the bench, yearning for the opportunity to play—not fearing injury. Strode was an excellent pass catcher at UCLA, but the Rams relegated him primarily to defense, perhaps in the hope that he would become further discouraged, and possibly injured. Weighing only 210 pounds Strode went up against National Football League linemen who weighed 250 pounds or more, yet he never backed down. If the Rams coaching staff and management thought he would be injured or quit the team, they underestimated both his strength and athletic ability, but more importantly his courage and tenacity.

The Los Angeles Rams finished the 1946 season with a disappointing record of 6-4-1. Washington, who saw limited action during the season, and Strode, who played even less, could not be blamed for the Rams' performance on the field. Regarding his nonuse by the Rams coaching staff, Strode noted:

At first I didn't feel bad; I just felt embarrassed. I resigned myself to the situation. I was making more money than I had with Schissler and I wasn't getting banged up. I was in the NFL and that was like a prize. . . . I proved I could play, but for whatever reason the Rams weren't interested in using me.

When somebody broke down, or they couldn't find anybody with guts enough to go out there and do the job, they'd stick me in and I would shine. But in my generation, players never defended their right to play. We just tried to prove ourselves in practice, which I did.[18]

The final statistics for Washington and Strode illustrated their limited use during the 1946 season. Washington finished the season with only 23 rushing attempts, gained 114 yards, averaged 5.0 yards per carry, and scored one touchdown. The Rams' leading rusher was Fred Gehrke, who, like Washington, played halfback. Gehrke finished with 71 rushing attempts, gained 371 yards, averaged 5.2 yards per carry, and scored three touchdowns. The numbers imply that if Washington had received as many carries as Gehrke he may have rushed for similar yardage and touchdowns. Strode caught only 4 passes for 37 yards, which gave him a 9.0 average yards per catch with no touchdowns and he returned one kickoff for 6 yards.

Although Washington and Strode did not have a big impact on the field, the Rams and the NFL enjoyed one of their most prosperous seasons in 1946. That year NFL games averaged 31,493 in paid attendance, the highest it had ever been, and it would remain the highest average total until the 1955 season. In 1946 NFL games set a weekly record for paid admission with a total of 208,882; Sunday November 10 was the first 200,000 attendance day for the National Football League. The largest crowd to attend an NFL game during the 1946 season consisted of the 68,381 people who witnessed the Chicago Bears play the Los Angeles Rams in Los Angeles. Although this was the largest crowd for the NFL, it fell below two crowds in the AAFC—both home games for the Cleveland Browns. On October 20 at Cleveland Municipal Stadium the Browns drew a crowd of 71,134, and another 70,836 attended on October 27.[19] It was not coincidental that the largest crowds to attend professional football games in the NFL and AAFC both involved home games of the Rams and Browns, the only two teams with black players. By 1946 both Los Angeles and Cleveland had substantial black populations, eager to watch fellow members of their race play major league sports.

Interestingly, the AAFC, viewed as an inferior league by the NFL, was more than able to compete for fans. During the 1946 season the NFL drew 1,732,135 in total paid attendance, and the AAFC 1,376,998. The eight teams that made up the AAFC in 1946 were: Cleveland Browns, San Francisco 49ers, Los Angeles Dons, New York Yankees, Buffalo Bisons, Chicago Rockets, Brooklyn Dodgers, and Miami Seahawks. The Browns drew more fans at home and on the road than any other team in the AAFC (Table 1). Arguably the Browns were the most important team in helping the new league to survive. Their on-the-field success made them the major drawing card of the AAFC, and that success can be attributed to the individual players themselves and to Coach Brown. More importantly, unlike the Rams of the NFL who used Strode and Washington as tokens, the Browns relied heavily on the athletic talents of Willis and Motley. Bill Willis played on the first team throughout the season, and Motley permanently joined the first team after the first few games. Both contributed greatly to the overall success of the Cleveland Browns in 1946.

In the first regular season game played in the AAFC, the Browns defeated the Miami Seahawks 44-0 at Cleveland Municipal Stadium. A crowd of 60,135 witnessed the game, with an estimated ten thousand black fans in attendance. Bill Willis was announced as part of the starting lineup, and received a standing ovation when he was introduced in the colorful pregame ceremonies. The black fans were thrilled to see the giant black man

Table 1

Attendance of the All-American Football Conference

HOME GAMES					
Team	*1946*	*1947*	*1948*	*1949*	*Team Totals*
Cleveland	399,963	390,939	318,619	188,947	1,298,468
San Francisco	182,198	239,217	287,183	234,192	942,790
Los Angeles	139,294	304,177	287,676	134,980	866,127
New York	194,140	264,412	166,864	144,659	770,075
Buffalo	117,954	217,699	176,197	160,430	672,280
Baltimore	—	199,661	206,109	152,381	558,151
Chicago	195,627	135,274	103,481	107,222	541,604
Brooklyn	97,671	77,101	72,497	—	247,269
Miami	50,151	—	—	—	50,151
Conf. Totals	1,376,998	1,828,480	1,618,626	1,122,811	5,946,915

ROAD GAMES					
Team	*1946*	*1947*	*1948*	*1949*	*Team Totals*
Cleveland	212,999	275,078	270,980	212,526	971,583
New York	173,915	334,005	216,557	171,515	895,992
San Francisco	157,278	248,855	256,161	213,628	875,922
Los Angeles	193,625	243,240	211,256	132,061	780,182
Buffalo	151,472	211,554	157,060	134,559	654,645
Chicago	155,649	166,892	164,262	127,924	614,727
Brooklyn	165,633	190,876	175,869	—	532,378
Baltimore	—	157,980	166,481	130,598	455,059
Miami	166,427	—	—	—	166,427
Conf. Totals	1,376,998	1,828,480	1,618,626	1,122,811	5,946,915[20]

trot out of the dugout and take his place alongside ten other teammates in the Browns' starting team.[21]

There was speculation before the game that acceptance of the two black players would not go smoothly, that possibly several of the Miami players who were from the South might take exception to playing against Willis and Motley. At the pregame practice session the day before the game, Seahawks Coach Jack Meagher responded to a reporter's question regarding some of his southern players' attitudes toward playing against the two black stars. Meagher replied, "They worked together in the army. Why can't they play together in football?"[22] After the game Willis and Motley reported no unnecessary roughness or dirty plays. The only negative incident followed Motley's great open field run in the second period for 23 yards. Motley thought he heard one of the Seahawks remark to a teammate: "Hey, boy, you want to get that black son of a bitch next time."[23] The frustration expressed by this white player was not isolated, and would be felt by many many more. For this was just the beginning of major changes that would sweep through the AAFC and NFL.

By the second game of the season it was very clear that in Motley and Willis the Browns had two of the best players in the AAFC at their respective positions. Fullback Marion Motley was a devastating runner and vicious blocker in the Browns' offensive attack. After their crushing defeat of the Seahawks, the Browns played the Chicago Rockets the following week. In that game Motley ran for 122 yards on 12 attempts, which also included a 20-yard touchdown run. He averaged slightly better than 10 yards per carry against the Rockets, as the Browns won 20-6. However, he had to leave the game for fourteen minutes after being knocked unconscious while attempting to recover a fumble. The Browns' defensive line was anchored by Willis. Although while at Ohio State he had played tackle, Willis was moved to guard by the Browns. Willis felt the readjustment took longer than he anticipated, but by the end of preseason he was thoroughly acclimated to the new position.[24]

The Browns won their first seven games of the 1946 season before losing to San Francisco and Los Angeles, the only two games they lost all season. They had the strongest offensive unit in the league, led by quarterback Otto Graham who was the top passer in the AAFC, and Motley who finished second to Spec Sanders of the New York Yankees for the rushing title. Motley finished second to Sanders, however, primarily because he did not receive the same number of attempts as Sanders. Sanders rushed for 709 yards on 140 attempts with an average of 5.1 yards per carry, scoring 6 touchdowns. Motley rushed for 601 yards on only 73 attempts with an average of 8.2 yards per carry, while scoring 5 touchdowns. With Graham the Browns threw the ball a great deal, while also featuring Motley. Subsequently this balanced attack prevented Motley from having as many carries as Sanders. However, while Sanders played in every game for the Yankees, Motley was forced to miss a game not because of injury but segregation. Motley and Willis were forced to miss one game played in Miami to accommodate southern white "sensibilities."[25]

On December 2, the two black players were prohibited from accompanying their teammates to Miami for a game against the Seahawks. In 1946 the state of Florida prohibited integration, which included allowing blacks and whites to compete against each other. Brown felt that both Willis and Motley "handled this very sensitive situation with great dignity and understanding, both then and throughout that season, and they made it easier for other black players to enter professional football."[26]

Not everyone supported the Browns' organization's compliance with Florida's discriminatory policy. Cleveland Jackson, writer for the black *Call and Post*, criticized southern segregation.

He thought the Browns should have taken Willis and Motley to Miami and confronted the local officials. If Brown did not challenge these discriminatory practices, Jackson contended, quite possibly his reputation as a defender of equality might be questioned:

> If Willis and Motley are to be kept out of the Miami game, then let it be said that Miami officials kept them out. Should the pregame antics of frantic partisans frighten Brown into leaving his two stars at home, his stature as a great coach would be seriously impaired. The least that he could do would be to take Willis and Motley to Miami and have them ready for regular play.
>
> Let the southern folks expel the players from the field. . . . When they send out the local gendarmes to take Willis and Motley off the football field, every newspaper in the country will take up the hue and cry which will be heard around the world. There is everything to gain by taking the lads to Miami.
>
> So it is with Paul Brown. It isn't expected of him to solve America's race problem. That is an impossibility for a single man. But the American sports world expects Brown to follow a bold pattern in his post as a leader of men.[27]

Paul Brown and the Cleveland Browns organization did not heed the words of Jackson when they visited Miami. Both Willis and Motley had received death threats, and the Browns felt it was in both players' interest not to accompany the team. Although there was speculation that the team's play might be affected by the absence of two of its most important players, the Browns defeated the Seahawks 34-0.

The Browns finished the season with a record of 12 and 2, and played the New York Yankees for the AAFC championship. The Yankees entered the game with a record of 10-3-1. Included in the three losses were two at the hands of the Browns, which led many to wonder if the Browns could defeat a team in three consecutive games. On December 22, some forty thousand fans watched the Browns defeat the Yankees 14-9 for the AAFC championship. Motley was instrumental in the Browns' victory, as he scored a touchdown on a 1-yard run, and rushed for 98 yards on only 13 carries. Motley led all players in rushing for the game, including his season rival Sanders, who finished the game with 55 yards on 14 carries, and he too scored a touchdown for his team on a 2-yard run.

The 1946 season in professional football ended very differently than the previous twelve seasons had. Four black players, Washington and Strode of the Rams and Willis and Motley of the Browns, were given opportunities that had been taken away only a few years before. However, only the Browns can receive full credit for this accomplishment because they voluntarily signed Willis and Motley. The Rams extended their opportunity because of outside pressure and the desire to lease the LA Coliseum.

The black press considered the reintegration of professional football one of the top stories of 1946. Only the debut of Jackie Robinson with the Montreal Royals was regarded as more important in the sports field than the signing of Washington, Strode, Willis, and Motley. Many black Americans believed that desegregation on the sports field would promote the spirit of equality in other aspects of American life. Writer Wendell Smith believed that athletic success was an "effective slap" at "racial mobsters" because "they know they can't explain these accomplishments and achievements, and at the same time convince you that some people are better than others by virtue of their racial heritage."[28]

The accomplishments of black athletes in professional baseball and football had a direct impact on other sports as well. In the Negro Leagues, the Cleveland Buckeyes signed a white pitcher, Eddie Klep, for the 1946 season. However, Jim Crow affected this white American as it had always affected black Americans. Prior to an exhibition game between the Buckeyes and the Birmingham Black Barons at Rickwood Field in Birmingham, Alabama, Klep was approached by two Birmingham police officers as he worked out during the pregame activities and instructed to leave the field immediately. The officers told Klep's teammates, "We don't have no mixin' down here." When asked if Klep could remain in the dugout during the game, the answer was "No, he can't sit in the dugout or any other place with you. If you want the game to go on, get him off the field and out of them clothes, else there won't be a ball game out here." Finally, when Klep returned in street clothes to watch the game, he was ordered to sit in the whites-only section.[29] Klep only played for one year with the Buckeyes, but his mere presence on the team was a direct challenge to the age of segregation.

After the 1946 season the major question in professional football was, would other teams in the NFL and AAFC follow the lead of the Rams and Browns? Would all teams begin to actively solicit, scout, and draft black players vigorously? When would every professional team have at least one black player on its roster? At the end of the 1946 season black athletes were optimistic regarding the racial policies of professional football and baseball. Although Jackie Robinson had not reached the major leagues in 1946, he was having such an outstanding year with the Montreal Royals that the anticipation of the possibilities for 1947 seemed unbearable for many blacks. Many communities around America wondered whether Robinson would be given a legitimate chance to play in the major leagues.

Finally, the signing of black players in professional baseball and football coincided with changes in professional basketball. The National Basketball League added five new teams for the

5. First and Ten

The Early Years of Reintegration

While watching an AAFC game at Ebbets Field in 1947, Fritz Pollard recounted how blacks like himself, Paul Robeson, and Duke Slater were brought into the unstable NFL after World War I as star gate attractions. Once the league was on a sound financial footing, he noted, the remaining black players were shown the door by George Preston Marshall, Tim Mara, George Halas, and the other league owners. Pollard feared that the same pattern would develop with the new All-America Conference, which had taken the lead in integrating pro football voluntarily. Such fears, however, proved groundless as black stars in the new league became gate attractions beyond all expectations. This was illustrated in a key game played between the Cleveland Browns and the New York Yankees in November 1947. More than seventy thousand fans, including more than twenty-five thousand blacks, jammed Yankee Stadium to watch Cleveland's imposing fullback Marion Motley duel with the Yankees' diminutive halfback Buddy Young. The total attendance topped the pro football record established in 1925 when Red Grange and the Chicago Bears played the New York Giants at the Polo Grounds. Pro football owners could not ignore the huge turnout and the conspicuously large number of black fans.[1] However, integration in pro football was painstakingly slow, and a source of great frustration for black players. No doubt, for black players the integration process that began in 1946 was a significant accomplishment. However, by the end of the decade only twenty-six blacks had played in the NFL or AAFC. Many had only one-year careers, and were merely tokens on their respective teams. In essence, during the early years of integration in professional football black players lived a very precarious existence.

At the end of the 1949 season the Philadelphia Eagles, Pittsburgh Steelers, Washington Redskins, New York Bulldogs, Chicago Bears, Chicago Cardinals, and Green Bay Packers of the NFL had not integrated their respective teams. In fact, only three teams—the LA Rams, Detroit Lions, and NY Giants—had black players on their rosters. By contrast, in the AAFC only two teams—the Buffalo Bills and Baltimore Colts—were without black players.

Of all the teams that brought on black players during this period, none compared to the Cleveland Browns. The Browns, champions of the AAFC, did not wait for other teams to sign black players but instead continued to add black talent. In January 1947, the Browns signed Horace Gillom, a star performer for Paul Brown at Massillon High School, and then at Nevada University. Gillom led the nation in punting in 1946, and his signing gave the Browns another pass catching end. With Bill Willis and Marion Motley already on the squad, the Browns were quickly becoming the most colorful team in professional football.[2]

The success of the Browns and the contributions to that success of their two black players facilitated a bidding war between the AAFC and NFL over the signing of a young black halfback. In early 1947 rumors began to spread surrounding the signing of Claude "Buddy" Young to a professional football contract. Several teams were interested in acquiring the extremely talented twenty-one-year-old, five foot five inch 165-pound running back.

In his freshman year at the University of Illinois in 1944 Young scored thirteen touchdowns, tying Red Grange's all-time record in a single Big Nine season. In 1945 while in the service, Young played as a member of the Fleet City Bluejackets, champions of the service teams league. In January 1947, after returning to Illinois Young became the first black athlete to score in the Rose Bowl, leading the fighting Illini to a 45-14 rout over UCLA, scoring two touchdowns and gaining 103 yards. Although Young had played only two years at Illinois the Yankees and Dons of the AAFC were rumored to have an interest in Young along with the Rams in the NFL.[3] Initial reports in January had Young signing with the Yankees at a salary of $37,000 for two seasons, along with a $10,000 signing bonus. In February Don Ameche, actor and owner of the LA Dons, indicated he might pay Young $20,000 a year for his services. By late February reports hinted that the Yankees might offer Young $125,000 for three years with a $25,000 signing bonus.[4]

Amid all the rumors surrounding the signing of Young to a pro contract, he became indirectly involved in a scandal concerning heavyweight boxing champion Joe Louis. Young was one of a team of college players picked to participate in an all-star football game scheduled against players from the Pacific Coast Football League. The game was to be cosponsored by Louis and played in Los Angeles on January 31 at Gilmore Stadium. The game was not played because the stadium was never leased. Louis's manager, Miles Marshall, handled the negotiations for him, which included giving $7,500 to Harry Hall, a sports promoter. There was speculation that after taking a trip to Mexico and New York, Hall was unable to post the money to secure the stadium. (This was one of many bad investments by Louis that would ultimately lead to his financial downfall.) Hall appeared in court in late April to answer charges of grand theft, but the charges against him were dismissed.[5]

Although the college all-star game was never played, the rumors surrounding Young's signing continued. In early March, Dan Reeves, owner of the LA Rams, announced that he would not sign Young to a professional contract because an NFL rule stipulated that Young could only be signed after his class graduated in 1948.[6] So it appeared that the NFL was closed to Young unless he wanted to wait one full year, which he had no intention of doing.

The speculation surrounding the signing of Young, and for that matter everything taking place in the sporting world, became secondary to the accomplishment of Jackie Robinson. On April 15, 1947 Robinson played his first major league game as a member of the Brooklyn Dodgers. Robinson became the first black player to break the color barrier in major league baseball. This event captured the attention of America and forever changed the face of professional baseball. Although black players had been reintegrated into the NFL and integrated into the AAFC a year earlier, the attention given Robinson overshadowed the accomplishments taking place in pro football. In some ways this may have made it easier for black pro football players, in that they did not receive near the same media attention as Robinson. Although they experienced many of the same difficulties as Robinson, arguably the pressure of integrating pro baseball, then America's pastime, was itself far beyond comparison.

The rumors of Young's signing finally ended when it was disclosed that Dan Topping, owner of the New York Yankees, had in April signed Young to a three-year contract. Reportedly Young was to make in the neighborhood of $13,000 per season.[7]

Although Young's signing had preoccupied the media and fans, another black player, Elmore "Pepper" Harris had one month earlier signed a contract with the Brooklyn Dodgers. The signing of Harris was announced on April 26, just days after Robinson made his major league baseball debut, and Robinson's presence probably directly contributed to the signing of Harris. This was somewhat shocking because Harris was an outstanding track star and it was assumed he would participate in the 1948 Olympics. The national outdoor 400-meter champion and three-time winner of the indoor 600 meter was reportedly given a $10,000 a year salary by Freddie Frizsimmons, Dodger president. Although Harris was a key player on Morgan State's outstanding team of 1943, the former college halfback was signed primarily for publicity reasons.[8]

Thus by August 1947, several AAFC teams were extending black players opportunities to make their rosters. The Yankees had four black players in camp: Jack Kelly, halfback from Fresno State College; Archie Harris, end from Indiana University; John Moody, fullback from Morris Brown College; Buddy Young, halfback from the University of Illinois. The Chicago Rockets had three black players in camp—Bill "Smallmouth" Bass, halfback from Tennessee State and the University of Nevada; James Shepard, halfback from Texas College; and Bernie Jefferson, halfback from Northwestern University. The LA Dons opened camp with forty players, which included eight blacks: Talmadge Owens, end from Clark University; Ezzrett "Sugarfoot" Anderson, end from Kentucky State; John Brown, center from North Carolina College; Willie Peters, end from Santa Barbara State; Oscar Givens, quarterback from Morgan State; Bert Piggott, halfback from the University of Illinois; Charlie Price, fullback from Virginia State; and Pelican Hill, halfback from Southern A&M.[9]

However, although many black players were invited to several pro camps, only a handful were added to team rosters. The Yankees released Moody, Harris, and Kelly. The Rockets released Shepard and Jefferson, while the Dons cut Owens, Peters, Givens, Price, and Hill. In fact, by the beginning of September 1947, there were rumors that both Kenny Washington and Woody Strode were possible cuts by the LA Rams. Those rumors became partially true when the Rams released Strode in early September. Strode claimed that his biracial marriage, of which Rams management did not approve, caused his release. Washington, who did make the team, told Strode: "It's not your ability; it's your life style. Dan Reeves does not approve of your marriage to Luana and your Hawaiian life style."[10] Strode's frustration at being relegated to the bench by the Rams as a result of token integration, comes through clearly in his reflections on his experience: "If I have to integrate heaven, I don't want to go. I was shoved down their throats, and that made them mad, and they took it out on me."[11]

Strode was not the only black player released who felt his race was the driving force preventing him from making a professional football team. On October 25, a published report indicated that Archie Harris, former Indiana University end, was suing the New York Yankees team for racial discrimination. Harris claimed he was released because of his race and that the Yankees kept Buddy Young as "a box office attraction." Harris also claimed damages for injuries sustained in practice, which resulted in his no longer being able to play football. According to the story, Harris was asking $15,000 in damages. Apparently Harris may have either settled with the Yankees out of court or dropped the suit altogether, for there were no further published reports surrounding his suit.[12]

The release of Harris and Strode exemplified the new unwritten policy adopted by many pro teams concerning the acquisition of black players—that of token integration. The 1947 season saw only seven new black players make professional team rosters. In 1946 there were eighteen professional football teams in the NFL and AAFC. The total number of players in both leagues was 594 (NFL 306 and AAFC 288), with two blacks in each league. In 1947 there were still eighteen professional football teams, with the total number of players being roughly 664 (NFL 360 and

AAFC 304), with a total of ten blacks. The NFL Rams had Kenny Washington on their roster, while five AAFC teams had the following black players: Cleveland Browns—Bill Willis, Marion Motley, and Horace Gillom; Chicago Rockets—Bill Bass; Brooklyn Dodgers—Elmore Harris; New York Yankees—Buddy Young; Los Angeles Dons—Bert Piggot, John Brown, and Ezzrett Anderson. At the end of the 1947 season, twelve teams in professional football had no black players on their rosters; nine in the NFL and three in the AAFC.

Despite these limited opportunities, those ten black players did have a significant effect on their respective teams. Kenny Washington enjoyed his best season as a pro under new head coach Bob Snyder. Washington rushed for 444 yards on sixty attempts, and led the entire NFL in average yards per carry at 7.4, while scoring five touchdowns. In contrast, Steve Van Buren of the Philadelphia Eagles led the NFL in rushing, gaining 1,008 yards on 217 carries, with an average yards per carry of 4.5 and scoring thirteen league leading touchdowns. Van Buren became only the second man in NFL history to rush for a thousand or more yards. Interestingly, the numbers imply that had Washington received the same number of carries as Van Buren, he may have gained over a thousand yards as well. While Van Buren averaged one touchdown for every sixteen carries, Washington's average was one per twelve carries. The Rams finished the season with a record of six wins and six losses, and again missed the league championship game. The NFL champions of 1947 were the Chicago Cardinals who defeated Van Buren's Philadelphia Eagles 28 to 21. Although the 1947 Rams had a mediocre season, Washington had the longest run from scrimmage in the NFL, a ninety-two-yard touchdown run against the Chicago Cardinals on November 2. Washington, at twenty-nine years of age and after several knee operations, still remained one of the league's most dangerous running backs. An exciting runner in his prime,

Washington was deprived of his best years because of the color barrier. If he could have the longest run in the NFL during his second season well after his prime and after several knee operations, what accomplishments might he have had over the course of the seven seasons that were taken from him? But there is some consolation in that although he was denied the opportunity to play in the NFL while in his prime, he did eventually open the door for other black players to follow. One such player was Buddy Young, one of the first great black running backs to benefit from Washington's breaking of the color barrier.[13]

Young introduced himself to professional football on August 29 as a member of the College All-Stars, who played the 1946 NFL champion Chicago Bears, at Soldiers' Field. A crowd of 105,840, the largest in the stadium's history, witnessed the All-Stars defeat the heavily favored Bears 16-0. Young virtually stole the show by gaining 163 total yards. Although he did not score any touchdowns, his runs of 34 and 25 yards and a pass reception of 50 yards helped to set up scores for his team. Young was named the game's most valuable player. The five foot five inch "Bronze Bullet" clearly illustrated that he could compete against the best the NFL had to offer.[14]

Young's performance in the All-Star game was just a preview of what lay ahead for his opponents. He finished second to Spec Sanders in team rushing, while leading the Yankees in catches with twenty-seven. He finished second on the team in punt returns and kickoff returns. Young's outstanding rookie season helped the New York Yankees win the AAFC eastern division. Young had made the most of his opportunity to succeed in professional football, but sadly not all black players received the same chances for advancement.

For Bill Bass of the Chicago Rockets the opportunity to perform in professional football was short-lived. Bass played only one year for the Rockets at halfback. Bass rushed twenty-eight times, gaining 44 yards, averaging 1.6 yards per carry, and scored no rushing touchdowns. He completed his only pass attempt on the season for 14 yards, and caught 8 passes for 79 yards, an average yards per catch of 10, and scored one touchdown. The Rockets lost the first ten games of the season, and finished the 1947 season with a dismal record of one win and thirteen losses. The limited opportunities granted to Bass on the field are ironic in light of comments made by head coach Jim Crowley in early August. When asked to compare the abilities of Bass to those of Young, Crowley contended: "After several weeks of training and two intersquad games, we are happy to say that we are convinced Bass will prove a more valuable player to us than Young would have been. We don't mean to say that Young is not a great player. . . . We do mean to say that, in our opinion, Bass is an even greater prospect." Although Crowley seemed high on Bass and his abilities during the exhibition season, when the regular season began Bass spent most of his time on the Rockets bench. This scenario of limited playing time not only affected Bass but several other black players as well.[15]

Jackie Robinson's major league debut may have caused the Brooklyn Dodgers of the AAFC to place Elmore Harris on their team. The fact that Robinson was playing for the Dodgers baseball team likely pressured the football team's management to bring on Harris to offset any possible criticism. That this was their reason for hiring him is confirmed by the fact that Harris played only the 1947 season for the Dodgers. More accurately, Harris was on the team during the season, and not really given an opportunity to play. Harris was allowed only three rushing attempts for the entire season, for -2 yards, with an average of -0.7 yards per carry, scoring no touchdowns nor receiving any pass attempts. Finishing the season with a record of 3-10-1 under Coach Cliff Battles, the Dodgers had a difficult time drawing fans, and the organization lost money.

The story in Los Angeles was similar for the three black players on the Dons' roster—limited playing time. In 1946 the Dons and Rams both promised to grant black players the opportunity to play on their respective teams, a concession made for the use of the LA Coliseum. The Rams of course kept their promise, while the Dons did not. However, although it was a year overdue, Ezzrett Anderson, Bert Piggot, and John Brown were the first blacks to play for the Dons. Anderson and Piggot had short careers with the Dons, for they were released after the season. Brown played through the 1949 season, the last year of the AAFC, before the Dons merged with the Rams for the 1950 season.[16]

Under Coach Dud DeGroot, who was fired in mid-season, the Dons ended the season with a record of seven wins and seven losses. Yet the Dons finished second only to the Browns in attendance, drawing 304,177, a figure that only a handful of NFL teams could match. The impact of the three black players on the team probably helped attract black fans that otherwise may have stayed away. Black fans were conspicuous during the first game of the year, played in the LA Coliseum against the New York Yankees, and their black star, Buddy Young. The September 12 game drew 82,675 fans, many of whom came to see if the "Bronze Bullet" was as talented as the eastern press described. They immediately discovered that he was. Young's spectacular runs helped lead the Yankees over the Dons 30-14.[17] Interestingly, Young's success did not cause the Dons to truly utilize their three black players. Anderson was an end with excellent speed and sure hands, but only caught eleven passes in limited use. Piggot was a running back and Brown a lineman; both struggled for playing time during the season.

During these early days of integration although most of the teams with black players did not fully utilize their black talent, not all teams bought into this self-defeating philosophy. Two AAFC franchises that decided to make the best use of their black

Charles Follis, the first black professional football player. (Courtesy of the Pro Football Hall of Fame)

Charles "Doc" Baker of the Akron Indians followed Follis as the game's second black pro during the 1908 season. (Courtesy of the Pro Football Hall of Fame)

Henry McDonald with the 1917 Rochester Jeffersons. (Courtesy of the Pro Football Hall of Fame)

Fritz Pollard at Brown University, circa 1916. Pollard was pro football's first black coach and arguably its first black star. (Courtesy of the Pro Football Hall of Fame)

Paul Robeson as a member of the 1921 Akron Pros,
reigning world champions of professional football.
(Courtesy of the Pro Football Hall of Fame)

Above: Joe Lillard (#19) of the Chicago Cardinals as he returns a punt for a touchdown against the Chicago Bears on October 15, 1933. Beaten safety Red Grange (#77) leads the pursuit for the Bears. (Courtesy of the Pro Football Hall of Fame)

Left: Ray Kemp of the Pittsburgh Pirates in 1933. He along with Lillard were the last two black players to play in the NFL until 1946. (Courtesy of the Pro Football Hall of Fame)

Right: Woody Strode suited up with the 1946 Los Angeles Rams, but was never really given a chance to play. (Courtesy of the Pro Football Hall of Fame)

Below: Kenny Washington broke the NFL's color barrier in 1946. Here he breaks into the open field against would-be tacklers as a member of the 1946 Los Angeles Rams. (Courtesy of the Pro Football Hall of Fame)

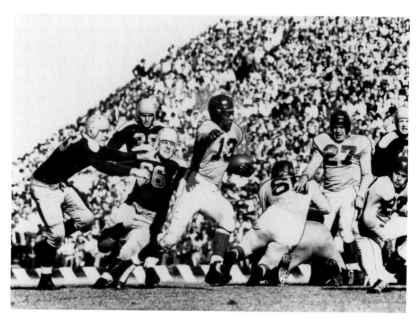

Bill Willis (#30) of the Cleveland Browns helps make a tackle in a game against the New York Giants on October 1, 1950. (Courtesy of the Pro Football Hall of Fame)

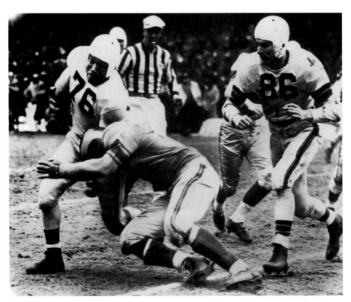

Still considered by many the greatest fullback to play the game, Marion Motley picks up tough yards against the Los Angeles Rams. (Courtesy of the Pro Football Hall of Fame)

players were the Cleveland Browns and New York Yankees, who not coincidentally dominated league play. The Yankees of the eastern division and the Browns of the western were the two best teams in the AAFC during the regular season. They met in the 1947 championship game, a game the Yankees had lost to the Browns one year earlier. The Yankees felt their team was substantially stronger with Young and they would repay the Browns for the previous year's lost championship. Young's accomplishments surely added to the Yankees' confidence, as he finished second on the team in rushing with 712 yards on 116 carries for an average of 6.1 yards per carry and scored three rushing touchdowns. He led the Yankees in receiving with twenty-seven catches for 303 yards, an average of 11 yards per catch while scoring two touchdowns. The Yankees had a powerful offensive tandem with rookie Young and running back Spec Sanders. Sanders led all of professional football in rushing with 1,432 yards on 231 attempts, an average of 6.2 yards per carry, while scoring eighteen league-leading touchdowns. The Yankees finished the season with a record of eleven wins, two losses, and one tie under Coach Ray Flaherty. But the Browns were responsible for one loss and the tie, leaving many to wonder if the Yankees truly could beat the powerful Browns.[18]

The Browns and the Dons had three black players, more than any other team in pro football, but that is where the comparisons ended. The Browns took full advantage of their black talent and this was the foundation of their success. Marion Motley bashed his way to 889 yards rushing on 146 attempts, averaging 6.1 yards and scoring eight touchdowns; Horace Gillom averaged 44.6 yards per kick on 47 punts; and Bill Willis anchored the Browns' defensive and offensive lines with a quickness that prompted many opposing players and coaches to classify him as the most difficult lineman to block in the league. The Browns possessed a lethal offensive attack that included the passing of Otto Graham and the receiving of Mac Speedie. Graham ranked as the best passer in the AAFC, leading the league in yardage with 2,753, completion percentage of 60.6, and touchdowns with twenty-five. Speedie led the league in receiving with 67 receptions for 1,028 yards, also scoring six touchdowns.[19]

The developing rivalry between the Browns and Yankees was attracting large numbers of fans. Arguably the black players on the Browns, Dons, and Yankees teams were specifically instrumental in the success of their attendance. In 1946 the Browns led the league in attendance, drawing 399,963, and again in 1947 with 390,939. Interestingly, the all-white Dons of 1946 were only able to draw 139,294, but the following year, with three black players, they drew 304,177 to finish second in attendance. The Yankees drew 194,140 in 1946 and 264,412 in 1947 to finish third in the league.[20]

The gate success of these three teams was the result of black fan support. This was never more in evidence than when the Yankees met the Browns in Cleveland on October 5. Of the 80,067 fans on hand to watch the Browns defeat the Yankees 26 to 17, an estimated fifteen thousand were black. In November, the Browns and Yankees met again, this time in Yankee Stadium; more than twenty-five thousand black fans watched as the two teams fought to a 28-28 tie. It was clear to all that black stars were enabling their respective teams to attract black fans in large numbers.[21] This factor alone would have seemed important enough to make all pro football owners actively solicit black players, notwithstanding the vast amount of black talent that could have helped many teams. However, most owners found it difficult to shed the policy of excluding blacks and in many cases their respective teams suffered.

The Browns and Yankees were again the only two teams in the AAFC with black players who played vital roles in the success of their teams; so it was no accident when they met in the season-ending championship game. Although played in New York as opposed to Cleveland the year before, the change in location did not change the outcome. The Browns defeated the Yankees for their second straight AAFC championship, 14 to 3. Motley and Young were the leading rushers in the game, with Motley gaining 109 yards on thirteen attempts for an average of 8.4 yards per carry. Young rushed sixteen times for 69 yards with an average of 4.3 yards per carry. Neither player scored any touchdowns, but each helped their team that day. The punting of Gillom and defensive play of Willis were instrumental in holding the Yankees without a touchdown. Gillom punted five times, with an average of 45.0 yards per kick, which kept the Yankees pinned down in their own territory. The defensive play of Willis helped bottle up the potent running attack of Young and Sanders throughout the game.

The AAFC existed for only two more seasons before merging with the NFL in 1950, yet during those years it never achieved total integration as a league. Only one other team in the AAFC brought on black players during this two-year period, the San Francisco 49ers in 1948. In the NFL, the Detroit Lions and New York Giants added black players to their rosters, but the handful of blacks in professional football were still concentrated on a few teams. The Lions brought on Mel Groomes, halfback from Indiana, and Bob Mann, end from Michigan. Emlen Tunnell, defensive back from Iowa, became the first black player for the New York Giants. Joe Perry, fullback from Compton Junior College, and Robert Mike, tackle from UCLA, were the first black players of the AAFC's San Francisco 49ers.[22]

The already integrated LA Dons, Chicago Rockets, and New York Yankees added several more black players to their rosters. Although the Dons cut Anderson and Piggott, they added Lin Sexton, halfback from Wichita State University, and Len Ford, end from Michigan. The Chicago Rockets let Bill Bass go and replaced him with defensive end Ike Owens from the University of Illinois. The Yankees brought on Tom Casey, halfback from Hampton Institute. Consequently, while in 1947 there were ten black players on professional football teams, in 1948 the number had increased to fourteen. Even so, during the 1948 and 1949 seasons black players were confined to the Rams, Lions, and Giants of the NFL and the Browns, Dons, Rockets (Hornets 1949), Yankees, and 49ers of the AAFC. In essence not every NFL and AAFC team was committed to integration during the 1940s.[23]

Sadly, the end of the 1948 season also brought to an end the career of Kenny Washington, as he decided to retire from professional football. Los Angeles Mayor Fletcher Bowron officially proclaimed December 12 "Kenny Washington Day." Although Washington had had three productive seasons with the Rams, he had been prevented from displaying his talents during the apex of his career. In many ways Washington still suffers from the injustice of exclusion, as arguably the NFL should have inducted both Washington and Strode in its Hall of Fame. It should have done so not because of their individual achievements as players, but because they opened the door to the NFL for all the black players who followed. They are truly two forgotten pioneers whose contributions to the NFL cannot be measured by statistics but must be recognized for their sacrifices.

By the end of the 1948 season the NFL was in direct competition with the AAFC at the ticket gate. Although the NFL classified the talents of many players in the junior league as inferior to their players, the AAFC was not inferior at drawing crowds. In 1947 the NFL drew 1,837,437 total fans and the AAFC 1,828,480, but in 1948 the NFL only drew 1,525,243 to the AAFC's 1,618,626. In 1949, the last year for the AAFC, both leagues would draw slightly more than a million fans. The Cleveland Browns and their ability to attract black fans were the major reason the AAFC was able to attract large numbers of fans overall.

For example, on November 6, 1948 there were 82,769 fans on hand at Cleveland Municipal Stadium to watch the Browns defeat the 49ers 14 to 7, making this the largest crowd to watch a professional football game. Approximately twenty-five thousand fans were black. They were there to watch the five black players labor for both teams, especially opposing running backs Marion Motley and Joe "the Jet" Perry. This crowd broke the old record of 82,675 set by the LA Dons and NY Yankees in Los Angeles in 1947. Clearly, in terms of economics black players had the capacity to generate revenue in large part because of the black fans' identification with them.[24]

Still, teams continued to handicap themselves by not extending opportunities to players regardless of race. In the NFL the Philadelphia Eagles, Washington Redskins, Pittsburgh Steelers, Boston Yanks, Chicago Cardinals, Chicago Bears, and Green Bay Packers had no black players in 1948. In the AAFC, which had more black players than the NFL, the Buffalo Bills, Baltimore Colts, and Brooklyn Dodgers remained all-white. The repercussions of such policies were felt directly by the Bills who played the Browns in the 1948 championship game in Cleveland. The Bills had never had a black player in training camp, and were in no hurry to integrate their team. However, Motley integrated their end zone three times for touchdowns. Motley scored on runs of 29, 31, and 5 yards respectively, to tie a team record for touchdowns in one game. He carried the ball fourteen times for 133 yards, an average of about 10 yards per carry.[25] This performance should have alerted nonintegrated teams that by disregarding an entire group of potential players because of skin color, they were only reducing their ability to compete.

However, in 1949 the seven NFL teams and three AAFC teams that did not have black players on their rosters continued this policy. Interestingly, even the teams with black players appeared to embrace a discriminatory policy concerning those players.

That policy was one of "stacking," or confining black players to specific positions. Of the twenty black players over the past two seasons, most were halfbacks, defensive backs, or ends. John Brown of the Dons was the only black center, and Horace Gillom of the Browns was the only black punter. Bill Willis of the Browns and Robert Mike of the 49ers were the only black linemen, besides Brown, in professional football.

Teams also preferred black players from white colleges or universities as opposed to historically black institutions. Only four players in the AAFC had last played for a historically black institution before coming into the league, and in the NFL no black player from a black college or university had played in their league. Most professional teams, especially in the NFL, felt that black college players lacked the talent to play professionally. Management and coaches may have also felt that black players from predominantly white institutions knew how to play with white players, while they were uncertain how black players from black schools would adjust to playing alongside white players. However, the most important reason for the failure to actively recruit black players from black colleges was that the white coaches and general managers felt that these players lacked the necessary athletic ability to be successful at the professional level.

The 1949 season marked an important turning point in challenging this notion, when Paul "Tank" Younger arrived in the NFL and quickly shattered any misconception regarding the inferior ability of the black college football player. Younger, who played fullback and linebacker at Grambling College, was signed by the LA Rams. As a freshman at Grambling, Younger led the nation in touchdowns with 25, and would score 35 more during his career—his 60 career touchdowns were a collegiate record. Younger was the first black college player drafted by the NFL. For the six foot three inch, 230-pound twenty-year old, making the team as a black player was pressure enough. But his Grambling coach Eddie Robinson stressed to him the importance of his success at the professional level to black college football: "Tank, this is a great opportunity for black college football. You're the most outstanding player in black college football. If you fail, it's no telling when another player will get an opportunity. They'll say we took the best you had and he failed."[26] Although he became an important asset to the Rams, the immediate solicitation of black college players did not happen. Black college players were not actively recruited by pro football teams until the creation of the American Football League in 1960.

Several other black players began their pro careers as did Younger during the 1949 season. Wally Triplett, halfback from Penn State, was signed by the Detroit Lions. In the AAFC James Bailey, guard from West Virginia, joined the Chicago Hornets. The Rockets had been sold to new owners who changed the franchise's name to Hornets. However, the new owners still retained the policy of having only one black player on its team roster, as Ike Owens was cut and Bailey placed on the team. Likewise, the Yankees replaced Tom Casey with Sherman Howard of Nevada-Reno. Like Casey, Howard was a halfback. On the other hand, the Dons increased the number of blacks on their team from three to four. They released Lin Sexton, and brought on George Taliaferro, halfback/quarterback from Indiana University, along with Ben Whaley, guard from Virginia State.

At the end of the 1949 season the Browns once again finished as AAFC champions, but their season was not over. The AAFC scheduled a postseason game to be played in Houston, Texas, pitting the champions of the AAFC against a team of all-stars from other AAFC teams. The Browns and other conference teams with black players had investigated the possibility of a ban on black players since Houston was in the Deep South and was segregated. The investigator was told that "everything was settled" and any black players sent to Houston would play.[27]

Then, just when it appeared that racial friction surrounding the charity game in the segregated South had been alleviated, the game officials reported that no black spectators would be allowed into Rice University Stadium. When questioned about this development, Paul Brown, coach of the Browns, said, "There is nothing I can do about it. I wish there were. Well, someday maybe those people down there will wake up and see that they are just cutting their own throats by these silly prejudices."[28] Although Paul Brown felt that nothing could be done regarding the ban of black spectators, the Cleveland branch of the NAACP did not agree. The Cleveland NAACP wired the Houston NAACP, asking that action be taken to alter the situation: "Great interest here and throughout the Middle West on Houston's action in this instance. We know your militancy and therefore urge Negro citizens of Houston to demand accommodations. Wishing you great success in your drive for civil rights."[29] The pressure applied by the Houston and Cleveland branches of the NAACP forced Len McCarthy, a wealthy Texas oil man and sponsor of the game, to sell tickets to black spectators. According to Bill Willis, a considerable number of blacks bought tickets and witnessed the game. However, rain cut the total attendance to ten thousand. Willis, Motley, and Gillom played for the Browns, who lost the game 12-7 to the All-Stars. Joe Perry and Buddy Young were the lone black players for the All-Stars. The five black players were housed with private families while their teammates stayed in one of the finest hotels in Houston, owned by McCarthy.[30]

When the 1949 season ended, black players had made progress—albeit limited—in professional football. They continued to find themselves confined to specific teams as well as specific positions on those teams, forced in essence to compete against each other. For instance, blacks were primarily confined to various back positions both offensive and defensive, along with end and line positions. Positions such as linebacker or quarterback were strictly reserved for white players. But Fritz Pollard's fears that black players would be eased out of professional football after postwar stability was established proved to be unfounded. Black players' abilities and black fan support made it clear that owners could not afford to erect another postwar racial barrier. The upcoming merger between the NFL and AAFC caused much speculation regarding black players. Would the merger create new opportunities for black players in the 1950s? Or would the stubborn racial policies of most NFL teams dominate the league? Many black players hoped for better opportunities in the "new league" than they had had in the old one.

6. A New League with Old Rules

"The Golden Decade of the 1950s"

The sports arena was the first postwar battleground for blacks in their fight against racial discrimination. The high visibility of the professional athlete heightened African Americans' racial consciousness. By 1952 the NFL was in its seventh season of reintegration and major league baseball in its sixth season of integration. The American Bowling Congress had fought stubbornly to keep black bowlers out, but bowed to a court order in 1950, which told the organization to remove the clause in its constitution which restricted membership to people of the Caucasian race. The National Basketball Association color barrier was broken in 1950, when the Boston Celtics drafted their first black player, Charles "Chuck" Cooper. Althea Gibson was the first black woman to participate in the USLTA national singles tournament at Forest Hills in 1950. In 1951 she was the first to play at Wimbledon, and in 1957 she became the first to win a title at Wimbledon. In ice hockey, in 1950 Arthur Dorrington became the first black hockey player in America when he was signed by the Atlantic City Seagulls of the Eastern Amateur League. And the National Hockey League was integrated in 1957 when the Boston Bruins called up Willie O'Ree from its farm team. Finally, led by Joe Louis, black golfers caused the Professional Golfers Association to remove its restrictive clause in 1951. These accomplishments were significant, but there was still much work to be done. For black professional football players the merger of the NFL and AAFC created a "new league," albeit one with the same old rules of slow integration. Black players continued to trickle into the NFL in small numbers and remained confined to specific teams.

Arguably the 1950s were pro football's turning point, for it was during this decade that the NFL established itself as a major sports entity. This occurred as a result of two developments which began with the absorption of the AAFC, and culminated in the NFL's emergence as a television attraction. The 1950s saw the NFL enjoy unprecedented prosperity during this so-called "golden decade" for sports. However, the experience for black players during this period was one of struggle, limited opportunities, and an overall precarious existence. In essence during these years the integration of the league was a reluctant process.

In December 1949, NFL commissioner Bert Bell announced a merger of the AAFC and NFL. Although the Cleveland Browns, LA Dons, and San Francisco 49ers had been successes at the ticket gate, the other six franchises were not and all AAFC teams experienced a decline in attendance by 1949. The NFL added the Cleveland Browns, San Francisco 49ers, and the Baltimore Colts of the AAFC. With the exception of six players, the New York Yankees merged with the New York Bulldogs and scheduled home games in Yankee Stadium in New York. The Los Angeles Dons merged with the LA Rams, and the Buffalo Bills combined with the New York Giants. Only the Chicago Hornets were totally disbanded.[1]

With the merger, the NFL formed two conferences, the American and the National. The American Conference was composed of six teams: Cleveland Browns, New York Giants, Philadelphia Eagles, Pittsburgh Steelers, Chicago Cardinals, and Washington Redskins. The National Conference was made up of seven teams:

LA Rams, Chicago Bears, New York Yankees, Detroit Lions, Green Bay Packers, San Francisco 49ers, and Baltimore Colts. Each year the conference winners would meet in a championship game to determine the NFL champion.

During the last season of the AAFC, five of the seven teams had at least one black player, while the league had a total of twelve black players. Of the ten NFL teams in 1949 only three had black players, for a total number of five blacks in the league. Clearly, during its four-year existence the AAFC had extended more opportunities to black players than had the NFL. However, the NFL continued the reintegration process as America became involved militarily in Korea. Once again America called on African Americans to demonstrate their loyalty in a time of crisis, and once again the call was answered. However, as the Korean conflict was the first military engagement of black and white Americans after the desegregation of the U.S. armed forces, it generated some racial optimism among blacks across the country.

In this Cold War climate, the 1950 preseason began with no fewer than twenty-one black players vying for positions on NFL rosters. When the season began, the Browns still had Bill Willis, Marion Motley, and Horace Gillom; they added Len Ford, end from the LA Dons, and Emerson Cole, fullback from Toledo University. The LA Rams had only Tank Younger on their 1949 roster, but added Bob Boyd, end from Loyola; Dan "Deacon" Towler, fullback from Washington and Jefferson; Harry Thompson, guard from UCLA; and Woodley Lewis, defensive back from Oregon. The New York Yankees retained Buddy Young and Sherman Howard, and added George Taliaferro, who had played with the Dons in 1949. The New York Giants kept Emlen Tunnell and added Bob "Stonewall" Jackson, fullback from North Carolina A&T. The San Francisco 49ers and Detroit Lions only had one black player each on their respective rosters—Joe Perry and Wally Triplett. Bob Mike of the 49ers was released because of an off-the-field racial incident, and Bob Mann of the Lions was traded to the Yankees after refusing to take a pay cut. The Chicago Bears, Green Bay Packers, Baltimore Colts, Philadelphia Eagles, Pittsburgh Steelers, Chicago Cardinals, and Washington Redskins all began the season with no black players at all.

The release of Bob Mike by the 49ers typified contemporary race relations in America and the NFL. A college teammate of Jackie Robinson's at UCLA, Mike played tackle for the 49ers during the 1948 and 1949 seasons. On July 15, 1950 it was reported that Mike had been made the first black scout in the NFL. His responsibilities were to tour the South and East particularly in search of black players who he thought would make excellent additions to the 49ers. However, in September the 49ers released Mike, who also played both defensively and offensively at right and left tackles.[2]

Why had Mike been released? It was obvious that his value to the 49ers franchise was formidable. In an interview with black sportswriter John R. Williams, Mike attributed his departure to "the same old story . . . the race problem . . . but this time from a different angle." Mike explained that during the practice season, he had journeyed to the field in the company of a light-skinned black woman whom 49ers owner Anthony J. Morabito took to be white. Mike had not "the slightest idea that there was any concern, whatsoever, as to the racial identity of the woman until after he had been cut from the squad."[3] After learning the reason for his release, Mike took the woman to the office of the 49ers. Owner Morabito was embarrassed when Mike revealed to him that the supposed white woman was just another of America's many light-skinned blacks who are often mistaken for white. The incident created so much ill will between Morabito and Mike that the difficulty could not be bridged. In fact, after a heated exchange of words, Mike became so angry that it became impossible to heal the breach. The 49ers' official response to Mike's release, which came from coach Buck Shaw, was as follows: "Bob Mike was dropped because he wasn't good enough. . . . He wasn't showing any improvement. We have three new tackles who are better."[4] This was not the only off-the-field incident that caused a black player to fall out of favor with his team; a similar incident took place in Detroit with Bob Mann.

Mann was traded by the Detroit Lions to the New York Yankees after refusing to take a pay cut. Like Mike, he had been a major factor in his team's success during the 1949 season and like Mike his departure seems to have been rooted in an off-the-field racial incident. Even though Mann had led the NFL in 1949 with 1,014 yards receiving and had finished second with 66 catches, the Lions asked him to take a salary cut of $1,500. This would have reduced his annual salary from $7,500 to $6,000, only $2,000 above the minimum figure for NFL players. The Lions' explanation for requesting that Mann take a pay cut was "that the preponderance of player material and the merger of the two leagues prompted a general salary slash among players on all teams in the NFL." This was true; however, Mann's salary was not as high as that of other players, including players on the Lions roster.[5]

There was another possible reason behind Detroit's trading of Mann. During the summer of 1950, a black east side organization called Business Sales Inc. initiated a boycott of the Goebel Brewing Company when that company granted an east side distributorship to two long-term white employees. Representatives of Business Sales Inc. contended that a black firm should have been given consideration for the distributorship, since the delivery area was in a predominantly black section. Mann, who was an off-season sales employee of the Goebel Company, innocently became involved when it was erroneously reported that he had conferred with Business Sales representatives about the boycott and the distributorship.[6]

Black bar owners and businessmen refused to go along with the boycott when it was revealed that the Goebel brewery employed nearly three times as many black employees as any other brewery in the city. Without the support of black bar owners and businessmen, the boycott effort failed. However, unnamed sources felt that Mann's position in the matter was never cleared up to the satisfaction of Goebel officials. This was very significant in that the president of Goebel was Edwin Anderson, also president of the Lions. Mann was removed from the Goebel payroll on July 31, the date on which all Lion players departed for training camp at Ypsilanti.[7]

These two off-the-field incidents illustrate that although the black NFL player had reintegrated the league in 1946, his stay was by no means guaranteed by mere ability. Black players were supposed to be grateful for the opportunity to play in the NFL, and while in the league they were not to do anything that might jeopardize this limited opportunity granted by white owners and coaches. Bob Mike was not picked up by any other NFL team. Mann went from the Lions to the Yankees, but was released in September after playing a total of three minutes in exhibition games. Although he had very limited playing time he scored the only preseason touchdown for the Yankees against the Washington Redskins. Coach Red Strader said he released Mann because he was "too small" to make the squad. In early November Mann filed a complaint with the NFL, claiming that the league owners had made a "gentlemen's agreement" to keep him out of pro football. Mann felt that he had been classified as "undesirable" by league owners. Mann's charges were denied by Commissioner Bert Bell and the owners of the Lions. Bell asserted that he knew of no such "gentlemen's agreement" and said that he had never heard the player referred to as "undesirable" until he used the term himself. The blackballing of Mann ended when he joined the Green Bay Packers in late November, becoming their first black player. Mann played three more seasons for the Packers, where he led the team in catches in 1951 and finished second during his last two seasons before retiring.[8]

The Baltimore Colts broke their color barrier in the middle of the season, just as the Packers had. But this breakthrough came only after pressure from the black press. On October 7 Sam Lacy published an interview with Colt President Abe Watner in the *New Jersey Afro-American.* Apparently, many blacks in Baltimore had bought season tickets after Watner expressed "genuine interest in bringing on colored talent" for the upcoming season. However, the Colts did not take a black player to their Westminster, Maryland, training camp. Questioned about this and about his failure to live up to the pledge he had made during the summer, Watner replied that the club had been unable to obtain a suitable player. Watner said he wanted Marion Motley, George Taliaferro, or Buddy Young, but felt the only way to acquire them was through a trade, and at the present time they could not arrange a trade with anybody.[9]

In an October 7 editorial, Lacy wrote that "there isn't a pro team in football that wouldn't want any of the fellows he named. But as badly as the Colts need help, it doesn't seem plausible that the only players acceptable to them would be the three men who are among the best in the game."[10] Watner's response was that "there just isn't any other man available." Watner claimed ignorance of the fact that players such as Bob Mann, who had led the NFL in yardage the previous year, and John Brown, a veteran lineman of three years with the LA Dons, were available. Watner's response to Lacy's inquiries was that they "were well fortified in the matter of ends. Furthermore, that would be a matter for our coach, Clem Crowe, to decide."[11]

Two weeks later the Colts signed Ollie "Art" Fletcher, a twenty-five-year-old end from Washburn College, to a pro contract, making him their first black player. Lacy reported that contract terms were not disclosed, but he applauded the Colts for being the first professional team in the city of Baltimore to embrace a black player. Neither the Baltimore Orioles, baseball team of the International League, nor the Baltimore Bullets, members of the National Basketball Association, had ever fielded a team with a black performer. The six foot, four inch, 210-pound end made his Colt debut in a 24-14 loss to the Philadelphia Eagles on October 15. Fletcher was primarily used on defense because he arrived at practice only two days before the game.[12]

However, the signing of Fletcher was not without repercussions. Watner reported to Lacy that the signing "brought a flood of blasphemous telegrams, letters, and phone calls" from indignant white people who "cussed me out for, as they put it, trying to change the Maryland way of life." Some of them, Watner continued, "warned me that for every additional colored fan the Colts picked up as a result of the move, we would lose ten white patrons."[13] The Baltimore Colts finished the 1950 season with a disastrous record of one win and eleven losses. Attendance dwindled throughout the season, and the acquisition of Fletcher and the ensuing white boycott only helped seal the Colts' fate. Although white fans had threatened to stay away from games after the addition of Fletcher, the team, which had lost money for several previous seasons because of poor attendance, finally forced Watner to sell the franchise back to the league. The team was dismantled and the players spread around the league as part of a collegiate draft. Fletcher, however, was not signed by another team.

The total number of blacks in the NFL dropped during the 1951 season from nineteen to seventeen. The pale complexion of the Washington Redskins, Pittsburgh Steelers, Philadelphia Eagles, Chicago Cardinals, Chicago Bears, and Detroit Lions (Wally Triplett was drafted in November, and was not replaced by another black player) did not change during the 1951 season as they continued to field teams without any black players. Clearly, not all the teams in the NFL had made a firm decision to integrate. In fact, the NFL continued to play preseason games in the segregated South, not taking into consideration the ramifications of such actions on black players.

The Giants played the Redskins in Birmingham, Alabama, in an exhibition game in September. Unlike the Browns, who two years earlier in 1949 had refused to leave their black players behind after being invited to a Texas all-star game, the Giants allowed Emlen Tunnell and Bob Jackson to be barred from the game. The Birmingham NAACP became involved in the incident, issuing a statement that placed the blame on Coach Steve Owen, first for permitting the game to be scheduled, and second for not refusing to play unless he was permitted to use every available player on the team. The game, which the Redskins won 14-10 and which may have had a different outcome with Tunnel and Jackson, was sponsored by the Junior Chamber of Commerce and the proceeds went to the all-white Childrens' Hospital. According to a resolution adopted by the NAACP, Birmingham had no ordinance forbidding black and white players from participating in the same athletic contests. But city officials were instrumental in excluding Tunnell and Jackson from the game.[14] This policy of playing exhibition games in segregated cities by NFL teams continued to be problematic, but not enough for the league to stop doing it. Cities compensated teams well, so much so that this took precedence over the effects of segregation on black players. For some teams, such as the Redskins who made it a point to solicit white southern fans, financial compensation was a priority. The NFL's attempt to expand into the segregated South the following season was a natural progression of this priority.

In January 1952 New York Yankees owner Ted Collins sold the team back to the league. Collins realized that the Yanks could not compete with the Giants in New York. (He reported a loss of $1,500,000 over the last five years of the team's existence.) A group from Baltimore put in a bid for the Yanks, but the NFL did not believe the city could support pro football. Instead, the league accepted an offer for the 1952 season from a Dallas-based twenty-one-man consortium headed by Giles F. Miller and Connell Miller, sons of the founder of a Texas textile company, who named their new team the Dallas Texans.[15] Upon learning of the move, one of the first questions posed by the black press was what would become of Buddy Young, George Taliaferro, and Sherman Howard, who were now Texans. Would they be allowed to remain on the team or would they be sold? News reports speculated that the players would be sold and that no other black players would be added. It was also reported that if this occurred, teams with black players would not be allowed to participate against the Texans.

Young and Taliaferro were both enthusiastic when questioned about possibly playing in Texas. "I think it will be a fine thing," said Young. "Texas is a good sports area and the fans there are like the fans everywhere. If you give them something for their money, they will embrace you like they do anywhere else. I have no objection to going to Dallas, in fact, I'm looking forward to it with eagerness."[16] Taliaferro felt that Texas would be a welcome relief from Yankee Stadium, where the Giants had enjoyed more fan support. "Dallas has always supported sports. . . . I think it will be a good thing for the team, the league, and the players . . . but I'm sure that anybody who delivers will be as acceptable to Texas fans as he is to fans elsewhere."[17] Although both players were looking forward to going to Texas the final decision rested with the owners. Naturally they wanted the team to make money and had to consider the negative ramifications that the black players could have on the franchise. However, in late January it became official that the Texans planned to keep Young and Taliaferro but not Howard. After leading the Yankees in scoring and touch-downs the two previous seasons, Howard felt he was due a raise. Management did not acquiesce, and Howard was traded to the Browns for three players in late June.[18]

The Dallas Texans did not fare any better than the former Yan-kees, finishing the 1952 season with a record of one win and eleven losses. They suffered even more at the ticket gate than on the field, losing money because of very poor fan attendance. The Texans played their home games in Dallas's Cotton Bowl. But in four home games they attracted under fifty thousand in com-bined attendance. The owners reported to NFL Commissioner Bell that white Texans' racial prejudice was the reason for the lack of support. White fans simply refused to accept Young and Taliaferro. The black press agreed with this explanation, but also cited treatment of black fans by Dallas State Fairground officials. The *Chicago Defender* described how Monday had been tradition-ally set aside as "Negro day" each October during the fair. Blacks could eat and enjoy everything except one or two shows which were closed on that day, but on all other days of the fair they were segregated or refused service. On Sunday, the day of Texans' home games, there was only one open ticket office for blacks lo-cated on the other side of the stadium. When black fans finally got inside the stadium they found that the seats allotted to them were in the end zone directly behind the goal posts. Some de-manded their money back and got it; others swore never to at-tend another game.[19] The promoters of the team probably had little control over the prejudice of fairground officials, but this treatment of black fans only further doomed the team at the ticket gate. As one upset black fan commented: "You know we don't have the choice of entertainment over the weekend as peo-ple do in the large northern cities. We would have welcomed the chance to support the Texans but we were not going to pay the price asked and be shunted behind the goal posts . . . we will be damned if we are going to support the Texans or any other club and get the treatment they dished out."[20] In late December, Commissioner Bell declared that if fifteen thousand season tickets could be sold in advance, the Texans would become the Baltimore Colts. Baltimore's fans came through, and the city met the fifteen thousand ticket goal fifteen days ahead of the established deadline of January 22. Carroll Rosenbloom, a clothing manufacturer, became the owner at a cost of $200,000. The Colts of 1953 had three black players on their roster, Buddy Young and George Taliaferro of the Texans, and Mel Embree, former Pepperdine end.[21] Segregation was a major factor in the failure of the 1952 Texans, and it subsequently enabled the city of Baltimore to gain a team.

The Texans were not the only team engulfed in controversy over racial prejudice. In early October 1952, Edwin Henderson, writer for the National Negro Press Association, urged black fans to boycott Washington Redskins' and Senators' games. Henderson felt that these two teams in particular had not shown any hint of fair employment practices for black ball players. The owners, Henderson charged, thought that black fans would continue to buy tickets regardless of the attitude of management toward black people. The owners grew richer because blacks flocked to games whenever a team with black players came to town. Although black fans wanted to see black players, Henderson now urged that they stay away until the policy changed.[22]

Although racial friction surrounded the Texans and Redskins throughout the year, the 1952 season ended with several teams integrating for the first time. The Bears' roster included their first black players, halfback Eddie Macon and guard Herman Clark. Halfbacks Don Stevens and Ralph Golston became the first black Eagles. Fullback Jack Spinks became the first black player for Pittsburgh since Ray Kemp. And halfbacks Ollie Matson and Wally Triplett (signed after fulfilling military duty),

along with offensive end Cliff Anderson, became the first black
Cardinals since Joe Lillard in 1933.[23]

The 1953 NFL draft saw a record thirteen black players selected by seven different teams. However, only halfback William
Anderson of the Bears, defensive end Willie Irvin of the Eagles,
and offensive tackle Roosevelt Brown who joined the Giants were
added to their respective teams' rosters. Also four undrafted
players made NFL team rosters. Defensive tackle Eugene "Big
Daddy" Lipscomb of Miller High School in Michigan played with
the LA Rams; halfback Willie Carter and defensive tackle George
Gilchrist, Jr., played for the Chicago Cardinals; fullback Leo
Miles made the Giants' roster; and the Chicago Bears signed
quarterback Willie Thrower of Michigan State. Thrower became
the first black quarterback to play in a regular season game in
twenty years. (The last was Joe Lillard of the Cardinals.) Thrower
made his NFL debut on October 18, when, with less than five
minutes to play and the San Francisco 49ers leading 35-21, Coach
George Halas allowed him one pass from the 49ers' sixteen-yard
line. The completed pass placed the Bears on the 49ers' four-
yard line. But then, strangely, Thrower was immediately replaced
by George Blanda, and did not see any more action; in fact he was
placed on waivers on November 7 and eventually given his outright release. Clearly the Bears never gave Thrower a legitimate
opportunity to display his talents. This was probably no accident.
The Bears were simply not ready to give a black player the opportunity to perform at the most important position on the field.
In 1953, black players in the NFL were primarily confined to the
backfield and line positions. George Halas and the Bears were
not going to become the first team to permanently change
league policy.[24]

By the end of the 1953 NFL season only the Detroit Lions,
Pittsburgh Steelers (Spinks was not resigned), and Washington
Redskins had no black players. George Preston Marshall, owner

of the all-white Redskins, told a Washington newspaper columnist in October that he would "like very much to sign a colored football player. But it seems the other guys always beat me to them."[25] Marshall continued to use this lame explanation, along with several others, whenever he was questioned about the Redskins' absence of black players. But it would become crystal clear that Marshall did not want any black players on his team. Not taking advantage of the best players available regardless of race only hurt the Redskins on the field. They would finish last for several years following the 1953 season which afforded them the number one draft choice, but they continually bypassed some of the best talent in college football out of self-defeating racism. However, in 1954 the Supreme Court issued a decision that called for racial change in education, which helped establish a new racial atmosphere which challenged old barriers.

On May 17, 1954 the Supreme Court declared segregation in public schools unconstitutional in its landmark case of *Brown v. Board of Education.* The decision was unanimous, and although it dealt with the narrow issue of segregation in public schools, it destroyed the legal foundations of segregation set forth in *Plessy v. Ferguson.* Black professional athletes had already integrated the playing fields of America, and this monumental Supreme Court case now justified integration in many other areas of American society, including the NFL.

But at the end of the 1954 season, two NFL teams, the Detroit Lions and Washington Redskins, still had no black players on their rosters. However, the 1955 season saw the Lions bring on their first black player, defensive tackle Walt Jenkins, since Wally Triplett had played during the 1950 season. Black fans were becoming more interested in the Lions because of the presence of three black players in the Lions' camp trying out for positions on the team roster. The Lions appeared to be sincere in giving the black players an opportunity to make the team because they took them along to various exhibition games in the Deep South, and allowed the players to participate in every game.[26] Subsequently, after the preseason Jenkins was added to the Lions' roster. Now only one team in the entire NFL still barred blacks from its roster, the Washington Redskins.

The acquisition of Jenkins by the Lions was a significant accomplishment during the 1955 season, but Charles Brackins playing quarterback for the Green Bay Packers was quite another. Brackins became only the fifth black player to play quarterback in a regular season NFL game. Fritz Pollard, Joe Lillard, Willie Thrower, and George Taliaferro had preceded Brackins, but all had received limited opportunities, and Brackins's experience was no different. Brackins had attended Prairie View A&M college in Texas, and was a sixteenth-round draft choice by the Packers. In college he had 534 passing attempts with 269 completions, for 3,485 yards. The Packers, however, only let Brackins play quarterback once during the season. On October 16, losing 41-10 to the Browns, Brackins was inserted with a few minutes left in the fourth quarter for starting quarterback Tobin Rote. Brackins threw only two passes, both incompletions, and although the Packers went on to lose the next two games, Brackins did not play again. Sportswriter Chuck Johnson noted that Tobin Rote was "the most inconsistent quarterback in football," yet it appeared that the Packers were not fortifying the position. On November 7, the Packers announced their plan to fortify the quarterback position, as they gave Brackins his unconditional release.[27] Again it was obvious that an NFL team was not quite ready to give a black quarterback a legitimate opportunity to play. Thrower and Brackins were mere premature experiments whose outcomes appear to have been predetermined.

Marion Motley's brilliant career also ended sadly in 1955, as he was traded by the Browns to the Pittsburgh Steelers. Motley never recovered from a knee injury, and was released by the Steelers in early November. Paul Brown, who described the trading of Motley in his autobiography, had hoped that Motley would have retired the year before: "I knew his days as a fullback were numbered. . . . Since Marion needed an extra year's salary to help him bridge a new career, we traded him to the Steelers. I didn't handle the situation well, because I didn't have the courage to tell Marion firsthand . . . and before I could think of a better solution, he found out from another source, deeply hurting him."[28] Although Brown admitted not handling the initial release of Motley properly, the Browns gave him no help once his career had officially ended. The Browns could have made Motley a scout, or assistant coach, or given him some other staff position, but this did not happen and Motley ended up as a clerk in a post office.

The 1955 season ended with approximately forty black players on various team rosters (except, of course, for the Redskins). This number represented an all-time high for black players in the National Football League. The next season, however, saw the number of black players drop to thirty-four, with the Detroit Lions falling back into the old all-white pattern. Jenkins was not resigned to a contract for the 1956 season. This pattern of adding and dropping black players probably kept a lot of the criticism that the Redskins received from being applied to the Lions. The Lions at least pretended that they had a genuine interest in acquiring black players, while George Preston Marshall, owner of the Redskins, did not. This was never more evident than during the 1957 NFL draft in January. The Redskins, who picked before the Browns and Baltimore Colts, did not select running back Jim Brown of Syracuse University nor offensive tackle Jim Parker of Ohio State. The color of the players' skins mattered more to Marshall than the fact that both players were All-Americans.

Although Brown grew up in the segregated South, he did not accept racial inferiority, and often questioned it. Brown emerged from Syracuse University with a noncompromising and con-frontational personality. One of the first inequalities that Brown noticed after entering the NFL was the low number of black play-ers in the league. The Detroit Lions continued their racist pat-tern of rotating black players on their roster yearly. For instance, John Henry Johnson, ex-49er, was the lone black Lion during the 1957 season. As Brown recalled, this was not unusual. In fact he observed a very visible pattern concerning black players on NFL teams:

> When I entered the NFL—1957—there was a quota for blacks. I doubt it was written, you probably couldn't prove it in court, every owner would deny it, but it was there. We always knew each team would have six, perhaps eight, blacks on a roster. Never seven though: it was always an even number, so none of the white guys would have to share a room with a black. Once [when] we went on the road, [we] had an odd number of black guys and an odd number of white guys; one of the black play-ers was back in Cleveland with an injury. Rather than pair off the extra black with the extra white, management bought each player a separate room. They were willing to pay for an addi-tional room in order to preserve the color line.[29]

There were even restrictions within the quotas. Brown quickly noticed the policy of "stacking." "Some teams would stack up three or four of their black guys at the same position. If a team had three black receivers, they'd stack them at one particular spot—typically flanker—so blacks wouldn't occupy all the re-ceiver spots. We'd see guys who were second and third string, running back punts and kickoffs, and know they should be start-ing across the board."[30]

The arrival of the brash Brown to the NFL in 1957 was not the only significant development that season. In January, Sam

Lacy once again took up the cause for black players by urging black fans to boycott Washington Redskins' games in reaction to revealing comments about ownership made by Harry Wismer, a minority stockholder in the team. Wismer, a TV broadcaster speaking at an annual dinner sponsored by the Capital Press Club, accused Marshall of antiracial policies in his operation of the professional football team. According to Wismer, he had once urged Marshall to strengthen his club with the addition of black college stars. "He told me," said Wismer, "You do the broadcasting and let me take care of running the team." Wismer went on to say, "I have heard it said Marshall has sworn never to have a colored player as long as he has anything to do with the Redskins."[31]

Lacy began to urge black fans to set up a picket line at Griffith Stadium during the football season. In February the D.C. branch of the NAACP sponsored a picket line that was maintained throughout the two-day meeting of the National Football League in Philadelphia. The line was led by Eugene Davidson, president of the D.C. branch, and Dr. Harry Greene, president of the Philadelphia branch. Other leaders included Matthew Adams, president, United Auto Workers, AFL-CIO No. 585; Joseph Ferrara, president, UAW-AFL-CIO Budd Local No. 818; Window Cleaners, AFL-CIO No. 125; Hobson Reynolds, head of the Elks Civil Liberties Division, and Dr. W. H. Gray, representing ministers.[32] The picket line succeeded in pulling these different organizations together. However, Marshall did not relent. The national branch of the NAACP suggested that if future pickets failed, a leaguewide boycott should go into effect against the Redskins.

Although Marshall and the Redskins gave no indication of relenting under growing protests, the Washington Senators did succumb to outside pressure. After the picket line, the Senators—who did not have a single black major league baseball player on their team—announced that Sam Hill, outfielder of the Birmingham Barons, would be brought to spring training for "special screening."[33]

On October 19 eleven picketers paraded around the entrance to Griffith Stadium to protest the Redskins' discriminatory hiring practices. The following week the number increased to eighteen. Inside Griffith Stadium the Chicago Cardinals were defeating the Redskins 44-14, with Ollie Matson the black halfback of the Cardinals running wild. He scored two touchdowns and totaled 155 yards on only thirteen carries.[34] Marshall's stance was firm in not integrating his beloved Redskins, even though his team's end zone was continuously being integrated by black players.

It is disturbing that black players themselves were relatively silent about this issue and other social and political developments of the late 1950s. Was this because of insecurity, or do other factors account for their political apathy? Rosey Grier, who was drafted by the New York Giants in 1955, described his state of mind at the beginning of his professional career as follows: "When I picked up a newspaper, it was to read the sports section. . . . Current events did not interest me. My world revolved around athletics, black entertainment, and my family. I had the dumb idea that as a well-known athlete, I ought not to get involved in politics because my voice would influence my listeners disproportionately. It was, of course, an insane rationalization for my self-protective and cowardly instincts."[35] Grier's thinking gives us some insight into the average black player's mentality, but the fear he describes was real in that by the late 1950s wholesale team integration, excluding the Redskins, was still decades away. Still, when the 1957 season ended there was a new all-time high of approximately forty-two black players on various NFL teams. The average NFL team had between thirty-eight and thirty-five players listed on its active roster. Thus, some eleven years after the reintegration of the NFL, black players were still only receiving a very limited opportunity to perform on the field, and none in the nation's capital.

The 1958 season saw a slight increase in the number of black players in the league, from forty-two to forty-nine. However, this number still did not include the Redskins. Lacy thus continued his criticism of Marshall, publishing an editorial in October in which he quoted Marshall as saying, "the only Jews and colored people he likes are those who buy tickets to Redskins' games." A press syndicate proposed that the team's name should be changed from Washington Redskins to Washington Confederates, because the bulk of the team's patronage came from Virginia and the Carolinas and the playing of "Hail to the Redskins" at home games was the signal for an outburst of rebel yells. Lacy was incredulous that black Washingtonians still continued to flock to Redskins games.[36]

Although Lacy was critical of black fans attending Redskins games, perhaps black fans went to see black players from other teams. Because, while Marshall continued to keep black players off his team, the Redskins continued to lose games because of outstanding performances by their black opponents. On October 4 against the Chicago Bears, rookie sensation Lenny Lyles of the Baltimore Colts brought a kickoff back for a 103-yard touchdown. In November, Lyles scored a 101-yard touchdown against the Redskins on a kickoff return, making him the first man in NFL history ever to return two kickoffs in the same year for more than a hundred yards.[37] Lyles was not the only black player who enjoyed success against the all-white Redskins. In nine games against the Redskins, Ollie Matson of the Chicago Cardinals scored eleven touchdowns; Willie Galimore of the Chicago Bears, playing in preseason and regular season games against Washington, scored nine touchdowns in four games; Tom Wilson of the LA Rams scored six touchdowns in six games; Jim Brown scored six touchdowns in three games, and before he retired, Marion Motley scored sixteen touchdowns against the Redskins' defense.[38]

Sadly, Kenny Washington and Marion Motley, two black players who had paved the way in 1946 for the reintegration of the NFL and integration of the AAFC, were both struggling financially by 1958. Their athletic careers over, Motley worked as a clerk in a Cleveland post office, while Washington was signed as a part-time scout by the Los Angeles Dodgers. These two men, who were important parts of the Browns and Rams respectively, were not given an opportunity to scout, coach, or work in their teams' front offices. In 1958 there were only three black scouts in professional football—Buddy Young of the Colts, Lowell Perry of the Steelers, and Em Tunnel of the Giants.[39] Of the two, Motley would have seemed to be the most likely candidate to be given a position with his former team. But despite the voluntary integration process that had become a legacy of the Browns, racial harmony did not prevail.

Yes, Paul Brown—without pressure—had played black players from the beginning, but that did not exonerate him from criticism concerning his treatment of black players. Jim Brown described this aspect of his coach:

> While Paul gave black players NFL citizenship, he didn't give them full citizenship. Blacks roomed together, we had a team quota. We all had the same rules, yet we didn't all have the same rules. . . . He said he never had a "racial problem" until I came to the Cleveland Browns. Apparently Paul thought everything was OK for the black Cleveland Browns in 1958. It wasn't. I don't want to belabor the point, but one man's racial problem is another man's equal rights.[40]

In 1959 the total number of black players in the league increased by only one, from forty-nine to fifty. However, the Redskins continued to remain all-white, thereby preventing total integration in the NFL. Ironically, major league baseball beat the NFL to the finish line of total league integration even though it began the process a year later. Jackie Robinson, who had retired from baseball at the end of the 1956 season, publicly criticized the Boston Red Sox for being the lone major league team without a black player, in early February. In July the Red Sox added Elijah "Pumpsie" Green to their roster, completing the integration of major league baseball.

Now the Redskins were the sole obstacle to the complete integration of the National Football League. In early January there were rumors that a players' delegation headed by Ollie Matson might picket the owners' sessions, protesting Marshall and his racial policies.[41] The picket line never took place, and black players probably hoped that a threatened picket would work just as well. But Marshall was a very stubborn and racist man who would not change his position easily. It would take more pressure than pickets or threatened pickets to integrate the Redskins.

Although the Redskins were not integrated in 1959, the creation of the American Football League that summer immediately created another professional football opportunity for black players, especially those who had not been given a legitimate chance in the NFL, specifically black players from historically black colleges. Most black players on NFL rosters came out of large white institutions, while black players at small black schools were often overlooked. Like the AAFC of 1946, the AFL, which was founded by Lamar Hunt, wanted to compete against the NFL for fans. The AFL did not have the luxury of being as selective as the NFL in choosing its players. And many black players who would have found themselves bypassed by the NFL, entered professional football via the AFL. In many ways 1959 was fourth and goal for black players in totally integrating professional football. They were about to enter into a new decade, a new league was on the horizon, and there was some optimism that Marshall was on the brink of relenting.

7. Touchdown

The Integration of the Washington Redskins

"We'll start signing Negroes," Washington Redskins owner George Preston Marshall once quipped, "when the Harlem Globetrotters start signing whites." In the twenty-five-year history of the franchise, no black had ever played for Marshall. Born in Grafton, West Virginia, in 1896, Marshall was raised in Washington, D.C. He dropped out of high school to pursue acting, but that career was interrupted by two years of service in World War I. Upon his father's death in 1919, he took over the family business: the Palace Laundry. As a businessman, Marshall displayed a knack for promotion through advertising. He developed the slogan "Long Live Linen," and by 1946, when he sold his company, he had transformed a small family business into a multimillion dollar chain with fifty-seven stores.[1]

In 1932 Marshall bought the Boston Braves, and to avoid confusion with the baseball team he renamed them the Redskins. Although blacks were not welcome on the team, Marshall hired "Lone Star" Dietz, a full-blooded Native American, as coach. In 1937, Marshall moved the team to Washington where the Redskins quickly became successful on the field and at the gate. Led by quarterback Sammy Baugh, the team won six division titles and two NFL championships between 1937 and 1945. After World War II, however, the Redskins failed to win another title under Marshall. The owner's stubborn refusal to employ black athletes no doubt contributed to the team's poor record. "Thanks to the Marshall Plan," lamented one sportswriter, the Redskins were "the whitest and worst" team in professional football.[2]

Although Marshall staunchly refused to play black players, the NFL as a whole enjoyed leaguewide success. In 1959 the NFL drew 3,140,409 paying customers, setting an attendance record for the eighth consecutive season, and generating tremendous profits for owners. Two Texans, Lamar Hunt, future owner of the Dallas Texans, and Bud Adams, future owner of the Houston Oilers, decided that pro football was ready for expansion. In 1959 Hunt and Adams founded the American Football League. Joining them was Harry Wismer, who owned 25 percent of the Washington Redskins and had been fighting a futile battle with Marshall over the hiring of black players. Wismer formed the New York Titans with backing from two Midland, Texas, oilmen. Wismer also brought in Ralph C. Wilson, Jr., who bought the Buffalo franchise. Of the eight AFL teams that began league play in 1960, the Houston Oilers, New York Titans, Buffalo Bills, Boston Patriots, Los Angeles Chargers, Dallas Texans, Oakland Raiders, and Denver Broncos all had at least two black players on their respective rosters. However, even though the new league was integrated on the field, there was segregation off it in Houston.[3]

Jack Scott, publicity director for the Houston Oilers, told the black *Houston Informer* that "members of the Negro press would not be included in the twenty-seven seat Jeppensen Stadium Press Box." Scott claimed that he was not segregating the press box, but rather that the twenty-seven seats had been allotted to persons they deemed "essential." Scott concluded by stating that he did not make the policy, but he was responsible for carrying it out.[4]

the 1952 NFL Dallas Texans who had segregated blacks, only to face heavy losses at the ticket gate and to fold after a year. In contrast, in their first home game at the Cotton Bowl the Texans had a crowd of fifty-one thousand on hand, of whom at least six thousand were black.[7] Although black fans were welcomed in Dallas, the black press was firmly committed to continue the pressure on the Oilers and their segregated seating policy, and on Marshall who seemingly had no intentions of integrating the Redskins.

Reporter Sam Lacy led a one-man crusade against Marshall and his resistance to integration. For years Lacy had written articles criticizing Marshall's refusal to bring on black players. Marshall never fully explained his position, but his southern origins no doubt contributed to his racism. He once claimed that he did not sign black athletes because white southerners on the team would have balked. That reasoning, however, had not dissuaded other owners from doing so. Marshall's desire for profits may have helped shape his position. As the owner of several radio and, later, television stations, he maintained that using black players would drive away advertisers and his white southern audience. Washington was a southern city that adhered rigidly to segregation during the 1930s and 1940s. During the 1950s, however, Washington gradually desegregated its schools, movie houses, theaters, churches, playgrounds, swimming pools, bowling alleys, restaurants, hotels, and public transportation system. Blacks joined the police and fire departments, the bar association, medical society, and nurses' association. Increasingly, blacks were hired by the federal government, and blacks were playing for the Washington Senators baseball team by the late 1950s.[8]

Despite these strides, racial intolerance and discrimination persisted in the nation's capital. Throughout the 1950s whites fled to segregated suburbs in Maryland and Virginia. In 1950 whites constituted about 65 percent of the city's population. Ten years later, whites were a minority at 45 percent. In 1960, six years after school desegregation, more than three-quarters of the public school population was black. Although blacks comprised a majority of the population, the city was governed by an all-white council appointed by the president. The police and fire departments had been integrated, but there were few black officers. Similarly, blacks were generally excluded from responsible positions in city government and business.[9]

In the 1960 presidential election black voter participation helped John F. Kennedy become president in the closest race ever. Kennedy received at least 70 percent of his support from blacks and Catholics. Willie Galimore, black running back for the Chicago Bears, endorsed Kennedy with a paid political advertisement in the *Chicago Defender* issues of October and November. Under Galimore's picture appeared the following statement: "What I want to see in the White House is a man who can score for our side. For my money, Kennedy's that man. He's not afraid to take a stand on fair employment, integration, and poll taxes. Senator Kennedy will do great things for our country and our people."[10] In November Gene "Big Daddy" Lipscomb, star lineman for the Baltimore Colts, also endorsed Kennedy: "He takes a stand and he speaks out for sit-in demonstrations, school integration, FEPC and voting rights, some pretty touchy issues in many parts of the country. Kennedy's like FDR—a real leader— not afraid to tackle tough problems. And that's why I'm voting for Senator John Kennedy for President on a straight Democratic ticket. You should, too."[11] These endorsements by Galimore and Lipscomb were representative of Kennedy's appeal to black voters. Throughout the campaign Kennedy chided the Republicans for not having done more to advance the cause of African Americans, and many blacks bought into his rhetoric.

So when John Kennedy moved into the White House in January 1961, African Americans had high expectations. As a presidential candidate, he had called for an end to racial discrimination through congressional legislation and strong executive leadership. In his first few months in office, JFK appointed more than fifty blacks to important positions. Yet he also named some white supremacists to the federal bench. During the campaign he had criticized President Eisenhower for not having put an end to discrimination in federally supported housing and declared that it could be done "with the stroke of a pen." However, Kennedy himself did not take that step until November 1962, two years after his election. In early March 1961, he issued an executive order creating the President's Committee on Equal Employment Opportunity. This newly created committee's first assignment could have been to examine the hiring practices of the Redskins across town who persistently refused to integrate.

The Redskins finished the 1960 season with a record of one win, nine losses, and one tie, which earned the team the number one draft pick. Still the Redskins did not deviate from their racial policy. They selected Wake Forest quarterback Norm Snead and nineteen other whites. Thirty-eight black players were picked as potential pros during the 1961 draft, spread among the thirteen current and future NFL teams. The Dallas Cowboys had just completed their inaugural season with four blacks on the team and selected three more in their first draft. The Minnesota Vikings, who joined the NFL in 1961, also participated in the draft and selected only one black player—Willie Jones, running back from Purdue.

After the draft, Marshall's critics came out in full force. Sam Lacy blasted Marshall's "lily-white stubbornness." "This column has never advocated suicide," he wrote in frustration, "but in George Preston Marshall's case, it would be readily forgivable." Pulitzer Prize-winning sports columnist Shirley Povich also took the owner to task. The Redskins' colors, he wrote, were "burgundy, gold and Caucasian." Finally, Gordon Cobbledick, a respected sports columnist for the *Cleveland Plain Dealer*, observed that the Redskins' Jim Crow policy was "spotting their rivals the tremendous advantage of exclusive rights to a whole race containing excellent football players." In the past, the Redskins had bypassed black athletes such as Jimmy Brown, Lenny Moore, Jim Parker, Roosevelt Grier, Roger Brown, and "Big Daddy" Lipscomb. "Drafting blacks," he cautioned, "is not an argument for social equality. It's a matter of practical football policy."[12]

Although the Redskins did not draft any black players, there was a positive trend developing for black players throughout the rest of the league. NFL coaches were beginning to respect players from historically black colleges and universities, schools whose play had traditionally been viewed as inferior to that of larger white institutions. Previously NFL coaches had tended to make their black player selections from white schools, but the 1961 draft saw eleven black players being taken from seven black schools. The AFL, which didn't have the luxury of overlooking black college players, actively sought black college talent. In fact, of the eight original AFL members, only the Los Angeles Chargers appear not to have begun with a black college player. The AFL would become a pipeline for many black college players into professional football, an avenue that otherwise would not have existed. However, as for the Redskins it was very obvious that Marshall would not integrate his team voluntarily. Interestingly, it was the federal government and not the NFL which challenged Marshall's racist policy. Fed up with Marshall, Secretary of the Interior Stewart L. Udall decided to move against the discriminatory hiring policies of the Washington Redskins.

Early in March 1961, Interior Department lawyers informed Udall that the administration might be able "to force Marshall's hand" on the color ban. They pointed out that he had recently signed a thirty-year lease to play all home games beginning October 1961, at D.C. Stadium, then under construction. Financed with public funds, the new $24 million stadium was located at

Anacosta Flats, part of the National Capital Parks system. As the "residential landlord" of the parks area, the Interior Department could deny use of the stadium to any party practicing discriminatory hiring policies.[13]

On March 24, Udall notified Marshall that the Interior Department had approved regulations prohibiting job discrimination to any party contracting to use "any public facility in a park area." At a press conference on March 28, Udall gave the Redskins a deadline for compliance. To avoid cancellation of the lease and possible criminal prosecution, Marshall had to comply with the administration's antidiscrimination policy by October 1, 1961, the date of the Redskins' first home game. Marshall could best show compliance by hiring a black player. Udall personally suggested that with a black player, Marshall's team "might win a few games."[14]

Marshall was initially caught off guard by Udall's ultimatum—"I don't know what the hell it's all about," he told reporters. He also attempted to laugh it off. "I never realized so many fans were interested in a football team that won only one game." Marshall also wondered why the federal government would get involved in what he considered such a "trifling matter." "I am surprised that with the world on the brink of another war they are worried about whether or not a Negro is going to play for the Redskins." He doubted that "the government had the right to tell the showman how to cast the play." Then he expressed a desire to discuss the issue with the president. "Yes, I'd like to debate that kid. I could handle him with words. I used to handle his old man in Boston." Finally, Marshall tried to downplay the charge of discrimination against the Redskins. "All the other teams we play have Negroes; does it matter which team has the Negroes?" The Redskins lacked blacks because they recruited players from segregated southern colleges. Recruiting southern white players was not a matter of prejudice, he declared, "but a business decision."

As for Udall's ultimatum, Marshall said that the NFL draft was over and his player roster was frozen. Leaving room to maneuver, however, he claimed that he was always open to the possibility of adding "players of recognized ability."[15]

By early August the pressure was mounting on Marshall and the Redskins. Journalist Brock Brockenbury of the *Los Angeles Times* reported that "George Preston Marshall and the Washington Redskins are in more trouble than they bargained for" when they arrive in the City of Angels for their exhibition game with the Rams on August 11. "In addition to pickets now being organized" to protest the Redskins all-white football team, a local group "is expected to seek an injunction which will prevent the unintegrated Redskins from operating in the LA Coliseum."[16]

The Redskins were not the only NFL team to be pressured on the issue of racial segregation. On August 10 the local chapter of the NAACP in Roanoke, Virginia, sent telegrams to three black players on the Pittsburgh Steelers and three black Baltimore Colts urging them not to appear in an exhibition game scheduled in the city for August 17. The NAACP disclosed that the local Chamber of Commerce had been accused of selling tickets to Municipal Stadium on a segregated basis. The Rev. R. R. Wilkinson notified Gene "Big Daddy" Lipscomb, John Nisby, and fullback John Henry Johnson of the Steelers, along with Lenny Moore, Joe Perry, and public relations assistant Buddy Young of the Colts that a suit had been filed in Federal District Court charging the promoters with using municipal property for the promotion of discrimination. The players were informed that picket lines would have to be crossed by anyone entering the stadium, players included.[17]

The picket line threatened by the Roanoke NAACP never materialized because NFL Commissioner Pete Rozelle stepped in and promised that there would be no segregated seating for the exhibition game. It is interesting that the commissioner felt compelled to step in and address the issue of segregated seating, but not the more pressing issue of integrating the Redskins. Although Marshall was the owner of the team and had the power to select the players he wanted or did not want on his team, the commissioner obviously had some responsibility regarding Marshall's racist policy. However, no sooner was the seating issue in Roanoke settled than the NFL faced another controversy, again led by a local chapter of the NAACP. On August 26 a planned exhibition game for Norfolk, Virginia, also faced possible pickets to protest segregated seating and the appearance of the all-white Redskins who were to face the Colts. Three local lawyers for the NAACP wired black players on the Colts asking them to withdraw from the game with the Redskins. The Colts sent general manager Don Kellett and his assistant, Buddy Young, to Norfolk the day before the game in the hope of working out a settlement.[18]

Both parties settled on an agreement that black fans would not be segregated. The game was played and the Colts defeated the Redskins 41-7. The promoters, however, insisted on retaining a Jim Crow section in compliance with a Virginia law. The NAACP countered this by arranging for the purchase of seats outside the specified black section. These seats were sold to local fans on a first-come basis. The local NAACP did, however, win a larger battle. After the game, management for the Colts made a pledge that they would never again be faced with the "unsavory task of playing in an atmosphere of discrimination. Having honored all contracts for the 1961 exhibition season, the club has no intention of ever entering into another agreement where the question of racial difference is likely to arise."[19]

As the Interior Department's October 1 deadline drew closer for Marshall and the Redskins, the public reaction to forced desegregation became evident, reflecting the deep divisions over civil rights in the 1960s. Outright racists, such as the American Nazi Party, paraded outside D.C. stadium with swastika-emblazoned signs reading "America Awake" and "Keep the Redskins White!" A fan from Tennessee believed America was headed for dictatorship "when a football owner is forced to put a nigger on his team."[20]

Despite some intense criticism, Udall refused to back down. The president supported his position, as did his brother, Attorney General Robert Kennedy and Secretary of Labor Arthur Goldberg. A longtime fan, Goldberg announced that he would boycott all Redskins games because their hiring policies were "an outrage and a disgrace." Many sports owners also supported the government's position. Bill Veeck, maverick owner of the Chicago White Sox baseball team, recommended threatening Marshall with the possibility of having an integrated AFL team play in Washington. William Shea and Jack Kent Cooke, members of the Redskins' Board of Directors, urged Marshall to yield. Edward B. Williams, who would become a stockholder in 1962, recalled Marshall saying "that under no circumstances would he change" his racial policy. Football owners, who had recently signed a lucrative television contract and dreaded the bad publicity of Marshall's intransigence, finally asked Commissioner Rozelle to mediate the conflict.[21]

Initially, Rozelle felt that the controversy was "strictly a club problem" and refused to intervene. But after being informed by Udall that the government would not back down and be pressured by other owners because of the negative publicity, Rozelle met with Marshall in late August and persuaded him to relent. Following the meeting, Marshall announced that his team had "no policy against the hiring of football players because of their race," that, in fact, he had prepared a list of five black players whom he planned to select, if they were available, at the annual NFL draft in December. Running backs Ernie Davis of Syracuse University and Larry Ferguson of Iowa headed the list. Marshall's conciliatory statement prompted a concession by Udall. He would permit the Redskins to field an all-white team at D.C. Stadium in 1961 if they agreed to place a black player on their roster the following year. Udall made it clear, however, that he was not backing down on his commitment to civil rights. "The Kennedy administration," he asserted, "is determined that every American should have a full and equal opportunity to utilize his or her talents in the classroom, in industry, on the playing field and in all areas of our national life."[22]

With the integration question seemingly behind him, Marshall settled back in to running his football team. He attempted to sign the Philadelphia Eagles to an exhibition game to be played at Norfolk, Virginia, during the fall of 1962. Marshall sent the Eagles a contract offering an exhibition booking at Norfolk's Foreman Field for September 1, 1962. The bid, however, was returned to the Redskins unsigned. General manager Vince McNally said the Eagles felt obliged to decline the invitation in "deference to their colored players—fullback Clarence Peaks and halfbacks Ted Dean, Tim Brown and Irv Cross." The four athletes said they preferred not to play before a segregated audience such as Virginia laws required. McNally said "further consideration of the Redskin invitation was immediately dropped."[23] This was a strong action by the Eagles. Obviously Marshall had no concerns about the segregated seating policies of certain cities—in fact he appeared to purposefully schedule games in these cities. Now for the first time a team took a stand against these policies and Marshall's solicitation of games in cities with segregated seating. However, the scheduling of exhibition games was the least of the Redskins' problems, for their performance as a team was simply terrible.

The 1961 Redskins finished with one win, twelve losses, and one tie, the worst record in the NFL. The second year Dallas Cowboys won four games and the first year Minnesota Vikings won three. The Redskins' lone victory and tie both came against the

Cowboys. The Redskins were also dead last in almost every statistical category—total first downs, rushing yards, average yards per rush; they scored a total of 174 points, with the next lowest team scoring 236 (Dallas).[24] In essence the Redskins had no real talent on their team, certainly not sufficient to compete adequately in the National Football League.

As the NFL draft approached, Udall gave Marshall a final warning. The draft, he declared, "is the showdown on this" and he expected Marshall to keep the promises he had made earlier in the year. With its abysmal record, the Redskins had the first pick on December 4. They selected Ernie Davis, running back from Syracuse University, the first black to win the Heisman Trophy. Two days earlier the Buffalo Bills of the AFL had also drafted Davis and there was some doubt as to whether Marshall would offer enough money to sign him. For their second pick, the Redskins chose another black halfback, Joe Hernandez from the University of Arizona. They also took Ron Hatcher, a black fullback from Michigan State, in the eighth round.[25]

In mid-December, Marshall divulged that on the day of the NFL draft he had secretly traded the rights to Davis to the Cleveland Browns. The Browns, who wanted Davis to join the league's leading rusher, Jimmy Brown, in their backfield, gave the Redskins two black players, Bobby Mitchell, an established running back, and Leroy Jackson, a number one draft choice. Several weeks later, the Redskins added another experienced black player when they acquired offensive guard John Nisby from the Pittsburgh Steelers. Ron Hatcher became the first black football player to sign a contract with the Redskins. When photographers at the signing asked Marshall to pose with the athlete, he refused, saying he did not wish to "exploit" the situation. As for the other black Redskins players, Hernandez never signed a contract, Hatcher and Jackson rarely played, but Nisby and Mitchell became stars.[26]

Thus the reintegration process that was initiated by the Los Angeles Rams with the signing of Kenny Washington and Woody Strode in 1946 was finally completed in 1962, when the Redskins' four black players took the field. One of the many questions posed to the players was, Did they feel added pressure, similar to Jackie Robinson? Mitchell responded, "I wasn't a Jackie Robinson." Although a pioneer, Mitchell downplayed the comparisons: "I wasn't quite as tough as Jackie. I would have loved to have just gone out on the field and played. . . . I was a little more sensitive, so those things affected me greatly—and I haven't forgotten them."[27] On the other hand, John Nisby didn't feel that the intense social climate affected his performance on the field: "You really aren't affected that much, because when you're involved in football, due to the demands of playing the game itself, you discipline yourself to do your job; you grow in developing that skill, and when you develop that skill you are performing at it, what the social, political, or economics may be around you become secondary."[28]

Both men also differed in their views of Marshall. Mitchell recalled being treated well by the owner. Marshall was "a nice man" who "never came across to me as a bigot or showed any behavior in that manner." Nisby was less charitable. "I never appreciated the man at all, because of the stand that he took on blacks prior to my arrival here. My relationship with the front office wasn't really that great."[29]

The start of the 1962 season signaled a new beginning for black Americans and black players in professional football. Pressure mounted by black sportswriters, fans, the NAACP, and the national government had forced professional football to complete integration on the field. By 1962, the NFL had abandoned cities like New Orleans; Columbia, South Carolina; Jackson, Mississippi; and Birmingham, Alabama, as sites for preseason exhibition games. The NFL was becoming increasingly conscious of the rising tide of black solidarity, and preferred to sacrifice the few extra dollars the teams would have picked up in those cities in order to harness the nationwide goodwill of 17 million African Americans.[30]

As many as ninety black players were on various NFL teams, and forty-seven on various AFL teams when the season began in 1962, but none were more noticeable than those on the Washington Redskins. In Washington's first game at Dallas, which ended in a tie, Mitchell ran back a kickoff for a 92-yard touchdown and scored on two passes. In the second game at Cleveland, he caught a 50-yard pass in the final minutes to upset the Browns 17-16. In the Redskins' third game, their first home game against the St. Louis Cardinals, Mitchell caught touchdown passes of 40 and 23 yards. Secretary Udall had accepted Marshall's invitation to be a special guest. After Mitchell's first score, Udall recalled the remarks of a black man seated behind him: "Thank God for Mr. Udall."[31]

The Rams came to town after the Cardinals, and were beaten 20-14 in front of 38,264 fans. The Redskins were atop the Eastern Division of the National Football League for the first time in years. The Redskins finished the season with a record of 5-7-2, the most wins since the 1956 season when they had finished 6-6-0. Mitchell led the league with eleven touchdowns, and caught seventy-two passes to earn a selection to the Pro-Bowl.[32]

Although Mitchell scored many on-the-field accomplishments, he "never felt totally accepted" by either blacks or whites in Washington, or the Redskins' alumni. "My problem with them," Mitchell recalled, "was that I knew I was performing quite well and I knew that I was the best thing that had happened to them in some time. And yet, I was not received in that manner away from the field. . . . I just wasn't accepted in the manner I felt I should have been by the people. And particularly the ex-Redskins. They just didn't quite open their arms to me."[33]

Mitchell had several successful seasons with the Redskins, and after his playing days became Assistant General Manager of the Redskins. Mitchell was elected to the Pro Football Hall of Fame in 1983. Nisby had three successful seasons with the Redskins and then was released over a salary dispute. In 1963 Marshall suffered a debilitating stroke and turned over control of the team to Edward B. Williams and Jack Kent Cooke. Marshall died in 1969. In his will, he left a sizable bequest to establish a foundation, named in his honor, to help improve the lives of disadvantaged youngsters of all races who resided in the Washington, D.C., area. However, there were rumors of a stipulation in Marshall's will about certain funds not going to blacks. And the uneasy feeling lingers among many that he was indeed a racist who simply found himself forced by the sociopolitical atmosphere of the times into hiring black players.[34]

Epilogue

The State of the Game

Given equal opportunity, black athletes' performances against their white counterparts could be judged on merit. African Americans seemed to sense that athletics represented one of the few areas in society where blacks could compete with whites under equal or nearly equal conditions. In his history of African American athletics, the tennis great Arthur R. Ashe, Jr., points out without too much exaggeration that early prominent black athletes "have been the most accomplished figures in the Afro-American subculture."

Some of the great black athletes of the past are still remembered and recognized by historians as symbolically important in the overall struggle for freedom, justice, and equality by African Americans. The names of Jack Johnson, Joe Louis, Jesse Owens, and Jackie Robinson are known and honored today. Johnson, Louis, and Owens competed magnificently before a world audience, while Robinson's integration of America's national pastime during the turbulent and tension-filled cold war years propelled him to lasting glory. Early black professional football players such as Fritz Pollard, Joe Lillard, or Kenny Washington were not in the same category as these paragons. Professional football was not international in scope—it wasn't even national. But it was this early obscurity that initially facilitated black participation in what was viewed as a minor sport.

Although the NFL initiated the reintegration process in 1946, it took seventeen years to complete. And it took another nine years for blacks to play at every position on a full-time basis. In 1960 black players made up only 5.5 percent of the linebackers and guards, while no blacks played regularly at center, kicker, punter, or quarterback. Black players were primarily confined to the running back, defensive back, and end positions. Institutional racism within the game facilitated by owners and coaches forced black players to be "stacked" at selected positions. Positions such as quarterback, linebacker, or center, which required more responsibility and thinking, were set aside for white players only. Black players were perceived as not being smart enough to play these positions, so the league once again established an unwritten policy that created a positional system of racial quotas and set-asides.

With the creation of the American Football League in 1960, black player participation in professional football increased dramatically. The new league created opportunities for many overlooked black college players that the NFL had regularly shunned. By the late 1960s, black players brought a new style of play to the football field, one born of pride in their accomplishments, an increased assertiveness because they were no longer tokens, and a rise in levels of self-esteem brought about by the black social revolution.

As of 1999, 68 percent of the players in the NFL are black. However, the one position on the football field that has remained largely closed to the black player is quarterback. Black players can be found in positions such as linebacker and center, but not at quarterback. The first black quarterback to play regularly was Marlin Briscoe, who in 1968 played for the Denver Broncos of the AFL. In 1969 Briscoe was changed to a receiver for the

Buffalo Bills, and he completed his brief four-season stay in professional football as a receiver. James Harris and Joe Gilliam followed Briscoe as black quarterbacks who played regularly in the NFL. Harris, who attended Grambling, played for the Buffalo Bills, Los Angeles Rams, and San Diego Chargers over the course of a twelve-year career beginning in 1969 and ending in 1981. He was the first black quarterback to possess any real sense of job security. Gilliam arrived in the NFL three years after Harris, drafted by the Pittsburgh Steelers out of Tennessee State, and played from 1972 to 1975.

When Gilliam arrived with the Steelers in 1972, the starting quarterback was Terry Bradshaw, who had been with the Steelers for two years and had thrown 19 touchdown passes and 46 interceptions. Despite these dismal statistics, Bradshaw remained the starter for the next two seasons. Bradshaw threw 12 touchdowns and 12 interceptions during the 1972 season and 10 touchdowns and 15 interceptions during the 1973 season. Gilliam was only given limited playing time while the Steelers allowed Bradshaw to struggle. During the 1974 season, Gilliam won the starting quarterback position and led the Steelers to a 6-0 preseason record. However, Gilliam was benched in favor of Bradshaw by midseason, even though he was ranked higher statistically as a passer than Bradshaw. The 1974 Steelers were loaded with talent—especially defensively—and they went on to win the Super Bowl, despite the quarterback position, which played a minor role in the team's success. In 1975 it was clear that the Steelers had made their choice as starting quarterback—Bradshaw played the bulk of the minutes, and Gilliam was relegated to mop-up duties. He found himself out of football after the 1975 season because of an addiction to cocaine that Gilliam says developed as a result of the constant pressure to succeed as a black quarterback.

The 1980s saw what many felt was a monumental breakthrough for black quarterbacks and their future. Doug Williams guided the Washington Redskins to the 1987 Super Bowl, becoming the first black quarterback to start a Super Bowl. While leading the Redskins over the Denver Broncos 42-10, Williams set several records: most yards passing in a quarter—228—four touchdown passes in a quarter, and most yards passing in a game—340. Williams was selected as the game's most valuable player. This performance should have answered the questions regarding the ability of black players to perform at the quarterback position. It was also in 1987 that Randall Cunningham became the starting quarterback of the Philadelphia Eagles. Cunningham was characterized as a quarterback with outstanding athletic ability, possessing the skills to pass as well as run.

In 1998, there were only six black starting quarterbacks among the thirty teams in the NFL: Randall Cunningham of the Minnesota Vikings (signed with the Vikings in 1996), Cordell Stewart of the Pittsburgh Steelers, Tony Banks of the St. Louis Rams, Steve McNair of the Tennessee Oilers, and Charlie Batch of the Detroit Lions. Why? In a league that is 68 percent black, only 17 percent of the starting quarterbacks are black. The answer to the question of whether the NFL has been truly integrated on the field is clearly no. One must then ask, Why are there not more black starting quarterbacks on various teams? Many NFL owners, general managers, and coaches would probably respond that there are only a few black quarterbacks in division one college football, and most are option quarterbacks—meaning that they are primarily runners instead of passers, which is the emphasis at the professional level. Therefore, they are usually changed to receivers or defensive backs once they arrive in the NFL. Arguably it is an unwritten fundamental policy, the same policy that kept blacks out of professional football for thirteen years, that black quarterbacks not be given a legitimate opportunity—unlike white quarterbacks. Many white owners, general managers, and coaches still want this position to remain primarily a set-aside for white players. The quarterback is the most visible player on the field, the most important, and is paid the most money.

Professional football on the field is integrated, except for the quarterback position, which is only partially integrated. However, when you look around the NFL at the various head coaches, general managers, and owners the numbers are even more disturbing. There are only three black head coaches—Dennis Green of the Vikings, Ray Rhodes of the Eagles, and Tony Dungy of the Buccaneers—and no black general managers or black majority owners. Are Dennis Green, Ray Rhodes, and Tony Dungy the only black men qualified to be head coaches? Of course not. But the fact remains that they were the only blacks to receive an opportunity in 1998. In 1996 there were eleven head coaching changes, yet none of the vacancies were filled by blacks. In 1997 there were four coaching vacancies, but once again none were filled by blacks. In 1998 there were two vacancies—the San Diego Chargers hired June Jones and the Oakland Raiders hired Jon Gruden. Sherman Lewis, the outstanding offensive coordinator of the Green Bay Packers, has arguably been the most qualified candidate over the 1997 and 1998 seasons. But he has been repeatedly passed over. It has to be his skin color, because any white coach with his credentials would already have been a head coach. He has earned Super Bowl rings as an offensive assistant with both the 49ers and Packers, and traditionally those are the first coaches chosen for team vacancies. After the Cowboys' Super Bowl wins in 1993 and 1994 both the defensive and offensive coordinators, Dave Wannstedt and Norv Turner, were given head coaching jobs with the Bears and Redskins. (Neither has been very successful.) But what makes this scenario upsetting is the fact that Gruden was an understudy of Lewis. Gruden spent the 1993 and 1994 campaigns as Green Bay's receivers' coach under the tutelage of offensive coordinator Lewis. There is no question that Lewis is qualified. Rather, the fundamental question is, how much have NFL owners really changed their racial outlook?

The game has come a long way since the days of Follis, Pollard, and Lillard. But the NFL has still not rectified the wrongs of the past and must deal with its present racial boundaries. The NFL can learn how to begin to do this from major league baseball. In 1997, in celebration of the fiftieth anniversary of Jackie Robinson breaking the color barrier, his number forty-two was retired by every major league team. Also, Larry Doby, who followed Robinson in integrating the American league but has been largely forgotten, was inducted into the Hall of Fame by the veterans' committee. Arguably the same should be done by the NFL with regard to the accomplishments of Follis, Pollard, and even Lillard. They all belong in the Hall not necessarily because of their on-the-field achievements but because of what they represent—the overall struggle and denial they had to endure. Many Negro League players have been inducted into baseball's Hall because of their contribution to the history of the game. The NFL must follow baseball and place these men where they belong. The color barrier lasted for twelve full seasons but this injustice has lasted much longer.

Undoubtedly, the challenge for African Americans and the National Football League going into the twenty-first century will be to fully integrate the coaching ranks and general managing positions, and become majority owners. The playing field has changed vastly since Follis, Lillard, Pollard, and Washington were first given an opportunity to play. However, in some respects it still remains the same.

Appendix

African Americans in Pro Football, 1904–1962

Player	Team	Years	School	Position
Pre-NFL Years				
Charles W. Follis*	Shelby Athletic Club	1904–6	Wooster	halfback
Charles "Doc" Baker	Akron Indians	1906–8 1911	none	halfback
Henry McDonald	Rochester Jeffersons	1911–17	Canandiagua Academy	halfback
Gideon "Charlie" Smith**	Canton Bulldogs	1915	Michigan Agr.	tackle
1920–1933				
Frederick "Fritz" Pollard	Akron	1919–21	Brown	back
	Milwaukee	1922		
	Hammond	1923, 1925		
	Providence	1925		
	Akron	1925–26		
Robert "Rube" Marshall	Rock Island	1919–21	Minnesota	end
	Duluth	1925		
Paul Robeson	Akron	1921	Rutgers	end
	Milwaukee	1922		
Jaye "Inky" Williams	Canton	1921	Brown	end
	Hammond	1921–26		
	Dayton	1924		
	Cleveland	1925		
John Shelbourne	Hammond	1922	Dartmouth	back
Fred "Duke" Slater	Milwaukee	1922	Iowa	tackle
	Rock Island	1922–25		
	Rock Island (AFL)	1926		
	Chicago Cardinals	1926–31		
James Turner	Milwaukee	1923	Northwestern	back
Sol Butler	Rock Island	1923	Dubuque	back
	Hammond	1923–24		
	Akron	1924		
	Hammond	1926		
	Canton	1926		

Player	Team	Years	School	Position
Dick Hudson	Minneapolis	1923	Creighton	back
	Hammond	1925–26		
Harold Bradley	Chicago Cardinals	1928	Washington	guard
David Myers	Staten Island	1930	New York Univ.	guard/back
	Brooklyn	1931		
Joe Lillard	Chicago Cardinals	1932–33	Oregon	back
Ray Kemp	Pittsburgh Pirates	1933	Duquesne	tackle

1946–1950

Player	Team	Years	School	Position
Kenny Washington	Los Angeles Rams	1946–48	UCLA	halfback
Woody Strode	Los Angeles Rams	1946	UCLA	end
Bill Willis	Cleveland Browns	1946–53	Ohio State	guard
Marion Motley	Cleveland Browns	1946–54	S. Carolina St.	fullback
	Pittsburgh Steelers	1955	Nevada-Reno	
Bill Bass	Chicago Rockets	1947	Nevada-Reno	halfback
Elmore Harris	Brooklyn Dodgers	1947	Morgan State	halfback
Buddy Young	New York Yankees	1947–51	Illinois	halfback
	Dallas Texans	1952		
	Baltimore Colts	1953–55		
Horace Gillom	Cleveland Browns	1947–56	Nevada-Reno	punter/end
Bert Piggot	Los Angeles Dons	1947	Illinois	halfback
John Brown	Los Angeles Dons	1947–49	N. Car. Central	center
Ezzert Anderson	Los Angeles Dons	1947	Kentucky State	end
Melvin Groomes	Detroit Lions	1948–49	Indiana	halfback
Bobb Mann	Detroit Lions	1948–49	Michigan	end
	Green Bay Packers	1950–53		
Joe Perry	San Francisco 49ers	1948–60	Compton J. C.	fullback
	Baltimore Colts	1961–62		
	San Francisco 49ers	1963		
Emlen Tunnell	New York Giants	1948–58	Toledo/Iowa	def. back
	Green Bay Packers	1959–61		
Lin Sexton	Los Angeles Dons	1948	Wichita State	halfback
Ike Owens	Chicago Rockets	1948	Illinois	def. end
Tom Casey	New York Yankees	1948	Hampton	halfback
Len Ford	Los Angeles Dons	1948–49	Michigan	def. end
	Cleveland Browns	1950–57		
	Green Bay Packers	1958		
Robert Mike	San Francisco 49ers	1948–49	UCLA	tackle
Paul "Tank" Younger	Los Angeles Rams	1949–57	Grambling	fullback
	Pittsburgh Steelers	1958		

Player	Team	Years	School	Position
George Taliaferro	Los Angeles Dons	1949	Indiana	halfback
	New York Yankees	1950–51		
	Dallas Texans	1952		
	Baltimore Colts	1953–54		
	Philadelphia Eagles	1955		
James Bailey	Chicago Hornets	1949	West Vir. St.	guard
Ben Whaley	Los Angeles Dons	1949	Virginia St.	guard
Wally Triplett	Detroit Lions	1949–50	Penn State	halfback
	Chicago Cardinals	1952–53		
Sherman Howard	New York Yankees	1949–51	Iowa/	halfback
	Cleveland Browns	1952–53	Nevada-Reno	
Ollie Fletcher	Los Angeles Dons	1949	U. Southern	guard
	Baltimore Colts	1950	California	
Bob Jackson	New York Giants	1950–51	N. Car. A&T	fullback
Bob Boyd	Los Angeles Rams	1950–51	Loyola	end
	Military Service	1952	Marymount	
	Los Angeles Rams	1953–57		
Dan Towler	Los Angeles Rams	1950–55	Wash. & Jeff	fullback
Harry Thompson	Los Angeles Rams	1950–54	UCLA	guard/
	Chicago Cardinals	1955		def. end
Woodley Lewis	Los Angeles Rams	1950–55	Oregon	def. back
	Chicago Cardinals	1956–59		
	Dallas Cowboys	1960		
Emerson Cole	Cleveland Browns	1950–52	Toledo	fullback
	Chicago Bears	1952		

1952–1955 (No new players in 1951)

Player	Team	Years	School	Position
Dick "Night Train" Lane	Los Angeles Rams	1952–53	Western Neb.	def. back
	Chicago Cardinals	1954–59	Comm. Coll.	
	Detroit Lions	1960–65		
Tom Johnson	Green Bay Packers	1952	Michigan	def. tackle
Eddie Macon	Chicago Bears	1952–53	U. of Pacific	halfback
	CFL	1954–59		
	Oakland Raiders	1960		
Herman Clark	Chicago Bears	1952	Oregon State	guard/
	Military Service	1953		linebacker
	Chicago Bears	1954–57		
Ollie Matson	Chicago Cardinals	1952	San Francisco	halfback
	Military Service	1953		
	Chicago Cardinals	1954–58		

Player	*Team*	*Years*	*School*	*Position*
Cliff Anderson	Chicago Cardinals	1952–53	Indiana	off. end
	New York Giants	1953		
Charlie Powell	San Francisco 49ers	1952–53	None	def. end
	Military Service	1954		
	San Francisco 49ers	1955–57		
	Pro Boxer	1958–59		
	Oakland Raiders	1960–61		
Jack Spinks	Pittsburgh Steelers	1952	Alcorn State	guard
	Green Bay Packers	1955–56		
	New York Giants	1956–57		
Don Stevens	Philadelphia Eagles	1952	Illinois	halfback
	Philadelphia Eagles	1954		
Ralph Goldston	Philadelphia Eagles	1952	Youngstown St.	halfback
	Injured	1954–55		
	Philadelphia Eagles	1954–55		
	CFL	1956		
Eugene "Big Daddy" Lipscomb	Los Angeles Rams	1953–55	None	def. tackle
	Baltimore Colts	1956–60		
	Pittsburgh Steelers	1961–62		
	(died of drug overdose on May 10, 1963)			
Roosevelt Brown	New York Giants	1953–6	Morgan State	off. tackle
Leo Miles	New York Giants	1953	Virginia State	def. back
Mel Embree	Baltimore Colts	1953	Pepperdine	off. end
	Chicago Cardinals	1954		
Billy Anderson	Chicago Bears	1953–54	Compton J.C.	halfback
Willie Thrower	Chicago Bears	1953	Michigan St.	quarterback
Willie Carter	Chicago Cardinals	1953	Tennessee St.	halfback
George Gilchrist	Chicago Cardinals	1953	Tennessee St.	def. tackle
Willie Irvin	Philadelphia Eagles	1953	Florida A&M	def. end
Maurice Bassett	Cleveland Browns	1954–56	Langston	fullback
Harold Bradley	Cleveland Browns	1954–56	Iowa	guard
Bobby Epps	New York Giants	1954–55	Pittsburgh	fullback
	New York Giants	1957		
John Henry Johnson	San Francisco 49ers	1954–56	Arizona St.	fullback/ def. back
	Detroit Lions	1957–59		
	Pittsburgh Steelers	1960–65		
	Houston Oilers	1966		
Chuck McMillan	Baltimore Colts	1954	John Carroll	def. back
Veryl Switzer	Green Bay Packers	1954–55	Kansas State	halfback/ def. back

Player	Team	Years	School	Position
Emmett King	Chicago Cardinals	1954	None	halfback
Burrell Shields	Pittsburgh Steelers	1954	John Carroll	halfback/
	Baltimore Colts	1955		def. back
Henry "Model T" Ford	Cleveland Browns	1955	Pittsburgh	halfback/
	Pittsburgh Steeler	1956		def. back
Tom "Emperor" Jones	Cleveland Browns	1955	Miami, Ohio	def. tackle
Mel Triplett	New York Giants	1955–60	Toledo	fullback
	Minnesota Vikings	1961–62		
Rosey Grier	New York Giants	1955–56	Penn State	def. tackle
	Military Service	1957		
	New York Giants	1958–62		
	Los Angeles Rams	1963–66		
	Injured	1967		
Jesse Thomas	Baltimore Colts	1955–57	Michigan State	def. back
	Los Angeles Chargers	1960		
Nate Borden	Green Bay Packers	1955–59	Indiana	def. end
	Dallas Cowboys	1960–61		
	Buffalo Bills	1962		
Charlie Brackins	Green Bay Packers	1955	Pr. View A&M	quarterback
Henry Mosley	Chicago Bears	1955	Morris Brown	halfback
Bobby Watkins	Chicago Bears	1955–57	Ohio State	halfback
	Chicago Cardinals	1958		
Dave Mann	Chicago Cardinals	1955–57	Oregon State	halfback/
	CFL	1958		def. back
Jimmy Hill	Chicago Cardinals	1955–57	Sam Houston	def. back
	Injured	1958	State	
	Chicago Cardinals	1959		
	St. Louis Cardinals	1960–64		
	Detroit Lions	1965		
	Kansas City Chiefs	1966		
Eddie Bell	Philadelphia Eagles	1955–58	Pennsylvania	def. back
	CFL	1959		
	New York Titans	1960		
Jack McClairen	Pittsburgh Steelers	1955–60	Bethune-Cookman	off. end
Willie McClung	Pittsburgh Steelers	1955–57	Florida A&M	off. tackle
	Cleveland Browns	1958–59		
	Detroit Lions	1960–61		
Walter Jenkins	Detroit Lions	1955	Wayne State	def. end

Player	Team	Years	School	Position
1956–1960				
Tom "Touchdown	Los Angeles Rams	1956–61	None	halfback
Tommy" Wilson	Cleveland Browns	1962		
	Minnesota Vikings	1963		
J. D. Smith	Chicago Bears	1956	N. Carolina	fullback/
	San Francisco 49ers	1956–64	A&T	def. back
	Dallas Cowboys	1965–66		
Lenny Moore	Baltimore Colts	1956–67	Penn State	halfback
J. C. Caroline	Chicago Bears	1956–65	Illinois	def. back
Perry Jeter	Chicago Bears	1956–57	Cal. Poly-Pomona	halfback
Julian "Sus" Spence	Chicago Cardinals	1956	Sam Houston State	def. back
	San Francisco 49ers	1957		
	Houston Oilers	1960–61		
Lowell Perry	Pittsburgh Steelers	1956	Michigan	off. end
Lamar Lundy	Los Angeles Rams	1957–69	Purdue	def. end
Jim Brown	Cleveland Browns	1957–65	Syracuse	fullback
Milt Campbell	Cleveland Browns	1957	Indiana	halfback
Frank Clarke	Cleveland Browns	1957–59	Colorado	off. end
	Dallas Cowboys	1960–67		
R. C. "Alley Oop" Owens	San Francisco 49ers	1957–61	Coll. of Idaho	off. end
	Baltimore Colts	1962–63		
	New York Giants	1964		
Jim Parker	Baltimore Colts	1957–67	Ohio State	off. tackle
Milt Davis	Baltimore Colts	1957–60	UCLA	def. back
Luke Owens	Baltimore Colts	1957	Kent State	def. end
	Chicago Cardinals	1958–59		
	St. Louis Cardinals	1960–65		
Frank Purnell	Green Bay Packers	1957	Alcorn State	fullback
Willie Galimore	Chicago Bears	1957–63	Florida A&M	halfback
	(died in auto accident at 1964 training camp)			
Herm Lee	Pittsburgh Steelers	1957	Florida A&M	off. tackle
	Chicago Bears	1958–66		
John Nisby	Pittsburgh Steelers	1957–61	Pacific (Ore.)	off. tackle
	Washington Redskins	1962–64		
Clarence Peaks	Philadelphia Eagles	1957–63	Michigan State	fullback
	Pittsburgh Steelers	1964–65		
Jim Jones	Los Angeles Rams	1958	Washington	def. back
	Oakland Raiders	1961		

Player	Team	Years	School	Position
Floyd Iglehart	Los Angeles Rams	1958	Wiley	def. back
John Baker	Los Angeles Rams	1958–61	N. Car. Central	def. end
	Philadelphia Eagles	1962		
	Pittsburgh Steelers	1963–67		
	Detroit Lions	1968		
Bobby Mitchell	Cleveland Browns	1958–61	Illinois	halfback
	Washington Redskins	1962–68		
Leroy Bolden	Cleveland Browns	1958–59	Michigan St.	halfback
Willie Davis	Cleveland Browns	1958–59	Grambling	def. end
	Green Bay Packers	1960–69		
Abe Woodson	San Francisco 49ers	1958–64	Illinois	def. back
	St. Louis Cardinals	1965–66		
Jim Pace	San Francisco 49ers	1958	Michigan	halfback
	Injured	1959		
	CFL	1960		
John Thomas	San Francisco 49ers	1958–67	U. of Pacific	off. guard
	Injured	1968		
Lenny Lyles	Baltimore Colts	1958	Louisville	def. back
	San Francisco 49ers	1959–60		
	Baltimore Colts	1961–69		
Sherman "Tank" Plunkett	Baltimore Colts	1958–60	Md. East. Shore	off. tackle
	San Diego Chargers	1961–62		
	New York Jets	1963–67		
Johnny Sample	Baltimore Colts	1958–60	Md. East. Shore	def. back
	Pittsburgh Steelers	1961–62		
	Washington Redskins	1963–65		
	New York Jets	1966–68		
Erich Barnes	Chicago Bears	1958–60	Purdue	def. back
	New York Giants	1961–64		
	Cleveland Browns	1965–71		
Joe Lewis	Pittsburgh Steelers	1958–60	Compton C. C.	def. tackle
	Baltimore Colts	1961		
	Philadelphia Eagles	1962		
Don Bishop	Pittsburgh Steelers	1958–59	LA City College	def. back
	Chicago Bears	1959		
	Dallas Cowboys	1960–65		
Proverb Jacobs	Philadelphia Eagles	1958	California	def. tackle
	New York Giants	1961		
	New York Jets	1961–62		
	Oakland Raiders	1963–64		

Player	Team	Years	School	Position
Dan Lewis	Detroit Lions	1958–64	Wisconsin	halfback
	Washington Redskins	1965		
	New York Giants	1966		
C. R. Roberts	San Francisco 49ers	1959–62	USC	fullback
Ellison Kelly	New York Giants	1959	Michigan St.	off. guard
George Scott	New York Giants	1959	Miami, Ohio	halfback
Timmy Brown	Green Bay Packers	1959	Ball State	halfback
	Philadelphia Eagles	1960–67		
	Baltimore Colts	1968		
A. D. Williams	Green Bay Packers	1959	U. of Pacific	end/
	Cleveland Browns	1960		flanker
	Minnesota Vikings	1961		
Lionel Taylor	Chicago Bears	1959	N. Mx.	receiver
	Denver Broncos	1960–66	Highlands	
Ted Bates	Chicago Cardinals	1959	Oregon State	linebacker
	St. Louis Cardinals	1960–62		
	New York Jets	1963		
Tom Barnett	Pittsburgh Steelers	1959–60	Purdue	halfback/
				def. back
Art Powell	Philadelphia Eagles	1959	San Jose St.	receiver
	New York Titans	1960–62		
	Oakland Raiders	1963–66		
	Buffalo Bills	1967		
	Minnesota Vikings	1968		
Dick Bass	Los Angeles Rams	1960–69	U. of Pacific	fullback
John Kennerson	Los Angeles Rams	1960	Kentucky St.	def. end
	Pittsburgh Steelers	1962		
	New York Titans	1962		
Chuck Janerette	Los Angeles Rams	1960	Penn State	def. tackle
	New York Giants	1961–62		
	New York Jets	1963		
	Denver Broncos	1964–65		
Prentice Gault	Cleveland Browns	1960	Oklahoma	halfback
	St. Louis Cardinals	1961–67		
Jim Marshall	Cleveland Browns	1960	Ohio State	def. end
	Minnesota Vikings	1961–79		
Jamie Caleb	Cleveland Browns	1960	Grambling	halfback
	Minnesota Vikings	1961		
	CFL	1962		
	Cleveland Browns	1965		

Player	Team	Years	School	Position
Ray Norton	San Francisco 49ers	1960–61	San Jose St.	halfback
Paul Winslow	Green Bay Packers	1960	N. Car. Cent	halfback
Willie Wood	Green Bay Packers	1960–71	USC	def. back
John "Bo" Farrington	Chicago Bears	1960–63	Prairie View	receiver
	(killed in auto accident at 1964 training camp)			
Charlie Bivins	Chicago Bears	1960–66	Morris Brown	halfback/
	Pittsburgh Steelers	1967		tight end
	Buffalo Bills	1967		
Tom Day	St. Louis Cardinals	1960	N. Car. A&T	def. end
	Buffalo Bills	1961–66		
	San Diego Chargers	1967		
	Buffalo Bills	1968		
Willie West	St. Louis Cardinals	1960–61	Oregon	def. back
	Buffalo Bills	1962–63		
	Denver Broncos	1964		
	New York Jets	1964–65		
	Miami Dolphins	1966–68		
Fred "the Hammer" Williamson	Pittsburgh Steelers	1960	Northwestern	def. back
	Oakland Raiders	1961–64		
	Kansas City Chiefs	1965–67		
Charlie Scales	Pittsburgh Steelers	1960–61	Indiana	fullback
	Cleveland Browns	1962–65		
	Atlanta Falcons	1966		
Ted Dean	Philadelphia Eagles	1960–63	Wichita State	halfback
	Minnesota Vikings	1964		
Roger Brown	Detroit Lions	1960–66	Md. East. Shore	def. tackle
	Los Angeles Rams	1967–69		
John White	Houston Oilers	1960–61	Tx. Southern	receiver
Bill Shockley	New York Titans	1960–61	West Chester	halfback/
	Buffalo Bills	1961		kicker
	New York Titans	1962		
	Pittsburgh Steelers	1968		
Ernie Barnes	New York Titans	1960	N. Car. Central	off. guard
	San Diego Chargers	1961–62		
	Denver Broncos	1963–64		
Howard Glenn	New York Titans	1960	Linfield	off. guard
	(died October 9, 1960—broken neck)			
Leroy Moore	Buffalo Bills	1960	Ft. Valley State	def. end
	Boston Patriots	1961–62		
	Buffalo Bills	1962–63		

Player	Team	Years	School	Position
Leroy Moore (continued)	Denver Broncos	1964–65		
Wilmer Fowler	Buffalo Bill	1960–61	Northwestern	halfback
Elbert Dubenion	Buffalo Bills	1960–68	Bluffton	receiver
Jim Sorey	Buffalo Bills	1960–62	Tx Southern	def. tackle
Monte Crockett	Buffalo Bills	1960–62	N. Mx. Highlands	receiver
Larry Garron	Boston Patriots	1960–68	Western Ill	halfback
Ron Burton	Boston Patriots	1960–65	Northwestern	halfback
Clyde Washington	Boston Patriots	1960–61	Purdue	def. back
	New York Jets	1963–65		
Walter Beach	Boston Patriots	1960–61	Central Michigan	def. back
	Cleveland Browns	1963–66		
Jim "Earthquake" Hunt	Boston Patriots	1960–70	Prairie View	def. tackle
George McGee	Boston Patriots	1960	Southern U.	off. tackle
	Military Service	1961–62		
Paul Lowe	Los Angeles Chargers	1960–61	Oregon State	halfback
	Injured	1962		
	San Diego Chargers	1963–67		
	Kansas City Chiefs	1968–69		
Charley McNeil	Los Angeles Chargers	1960–64	Compton C. C.	def. back
Ernie Wright	Los Angeles Chargers	1960–67	Ohio State	off. tackle
	Cincinnati Bengals	1968–71		
	San Diego Chargers	1972		
Rommie Loudd	Los Angeles Chargers	1960	UCLA	linebacker
	Boston Patriots	1961–62		
Dave Webster	Dallas Texans	1960–61	Prairie View	def. back
	Injured	1962		
Abner Haynes	Dallas Texans	1960–64	North Texas	halfback
	Denver Broncos	1965–66		
	Miami Dolphins	1967		
	New York Jets	1967		
Clem Daniels	Dallas Texans	1960	Prairie View	halfback
	Oakland Raiders	1961–67		
	San Francisco 49ers	1968		
Walter Napier	Dallas Texans	1960–61	Paul Quinn	def. tackle
John Harris	Oakland Raiders	1960–61	Santa Mon J.C.	def. back
Riley Morris	Oakland Raiders	1960–62	Florida A&M	linebacker
Charley Hardy	Oakland Raiders	1960–62	San Jose St.	receiver
J. D. "Jet Stream" Smith	Oakland Raiders	1960	Compton C. C.	fullback
	Chicago Bears	1961		

Player	Team	Years	School	Position
Gene Mingo	Denver Broncos	1960–63	None	halfback/
	Oakland Raiders	1964–65		kicker
Mike Nichols	Denver Broncos	1960–61	Ark. Pine Bluff	center
Chuck Gavin	Denver Broncos	1960–63	Tennessee St.	def. end
Willie Smith	Denver Broncos	1960	Michigan	off. guard
	Oakland Raiders	1961		
Jim Greer	Denver Broncos	1960	Elizabeth Cty State	receiver
Henry Bell	Denver Broncos	1960	None	halfback
Al Day	Denver Broncos	1960	Eastern Mich	linebacker

1961–1962

Player	Team	Years	School	Position
Deacon Jones	Los Angeles Rams	1961–71	South Car St.	def. end
	San Diego Chargers	1972–73		
	Washington Redskins	1974		
Elbert Kimbrough	Los Angeles Rams	1961	Northwestern	def. back
	San Francisco 49ers	1962–66		
	New Orleans Saints	1968		
Duane Allen	Los Angeles Rams	1961–64	Santa Ana J.C.	receiver
	Pittsburgh Steelers	1965		
	Baltimore Colts	1965		
	Chicago Bears	1966–67		
Pervis Atkins	Los Angeles Rams	1961–63	New Mexico St.	halfback
	Washington Redskins	1964–65		
	Oakland Raiders	1965–66		
Charley Cowan	Los Angeles Rams	1961–75	N. Mx. Highlands	off. tackle
Tom Watkins	Cleveland Browns	1961	Iowa St.	halfback
	Detroit Lions	1962–65		
	Injured	1966		
	Detroit Lions	1967		
	Pittsburgh Steelers	1968		
Preston Powell	Cleveland Browns	1961	Grambling	fullback
Charley Ferguson	Cleveland Browns	1961	Tennessee St.	receiver
	Minnesota Vikings	1962		
	Buffalo Bills	1963		
	Injured	1964		
	Buffalo Bills	1965–66		
	Injured	1967–68		
	Buffalo Bills	1969		

Player	Team	Years	School	Position
Roland Lakes	San Francisco 49ers	1961–70	Wichita St.	def. tackle
	New York Giants	1971		
Bernie Casey	San Francisco 49ers	1961–66	Bowling Green	flanker/
	Los Angeles Rams	1967–68		receiver
J. W. Lockett	San Francisco 49ers	1961	Central St.-OK	fullback
	Dallas Cowboys	1961–62		
	Baltimore Colts	1963		
	Washington Redskins	1964		
Jim Johnson	San Francisco 49ers	1961–76	UCLA	def. back
Pete Hall	New York Giants	1961	Marquette	receiver
Bob Gaiters	New York Giants	1961–62	New Mexico St.	halfback
	San Francisco 49ers	1962		
	Denver Broncos	1963		
Allan Webb	New York Giants	1961–65	Arnold	def. back
Bob Harrison	Baltimore Colts	1961	Ohio U.	def. back
Elijah Pitts	Green Bay Packers	1961–69	Philander	halfback
	Los Angeles Rams	1970	Smith	
	New Orleans Saints	1970		
	Green Bay Packers	1971		
Herb Adderly	Green Bay Packers	1961–69	Michigan St.	def. back
	Dallas Cowboys	1970–72		
Rosey Taylor	Chicago Bears	1961–69	Grambling	def. back
	San Francisco 49ers	1969–71		
	Washington Redskins	1972		
	Injured	1973		
Charley Granger	Dallas Cowboys	1961	Southern U.	off. tackle
	St. Louis Cardinals	1961		
Len Burnett	Pittsburgh Steelers	1961	Oregon	def. back
Wilbert Scott	Pittsburgh Steelers	1961	Indiana	linebacker
Irv Cross	Philadelphia Eagles	1961–65	Northwestern	def. back
	Los Angeles Rams	1966–68		
	Philadelphia Eagles	1969		
Amos Marsh	Dallas Cowboys	1961–64	Oregon St.	halfback
	Detroit Lions	1965–67		
Warren Livingston	Dallas Cowboys	1961–66	Arizona	def. back
Don Perkins	Dallas Cowboys	1961–68	New Mexico	fullback
Ray Hayes	Minnesota Vikings	1961	Central St.-Okla.	fullback
Bob Brooks	New York Titans	1961	Ohio U.	fullback
Moses Gray	New York Titans	1961–62	Indiana	off. tackle

Player	Team	Years	School	Position
Art Baker	Buffalo Bills	1961–62	Syracuse	fullback
Bob Kelly	Houston Oilers	1961–64	N. Mexico St.	off. tackle
	Kansas City Chiefs	1967		
	Cincinnati Bengals	1968		
	Atlanta Falcons	1969		
Mel West	Boston Patriots	1961	Missouri	halfback
	New York Titans	1961–62		
Bob Webb	Boston Patriots	1961–62	Iowa St.	halfback
	Injured	1963		
	Boston Patriots	1964–71		
Houston Antwine	Boston Patriots	1961–71	Southern	def. tackle
	Philadelphia Eagles	1972	Illinois	
Luther Hayes	San Diego Chargers	1961	USC	def. end
Bo Roberson	San Diego Chargers	1961	Cornell	flanker/
	Oakland Raiders	1962–65		halfback
	Buffalo Bills	1965		
	Miami Dolphins	1966		
Ernie Ladd	San Diego Chargers	1961–65	Grambling	def. tackle
	Houston Oilers	1966–67		
	Kansas City Chiefs	1967–68		
Earl Faison	San Diego Chargers	1961–66	Indiana	def. end
	Miami Dolphins	1966		
Charley Fuller	Oakland Raiders	1961–62	San. Fran. State	halfback
George Fleming	Oakland Raiders	1961	Washington	halfback
Jim Brewington	Oakland Raiders	1961	N. Car. Central	off. tackle
Buddy Allen	Denver Broncos	1961	Utah State	halfback
Al Frazier	Denver Broncos	1961–63	Florida A&M	halfback/ flanker
John Cash	Denver Broncos	1961–62	Allen	def. end
Dave Grayson	Dallas Texans	1961–62	Oregon	def. back
	Kansas City Chiefs	1963–64		
	Oakland Raiders	1965–70		
Bobby Smith	Los Angeles Rams	1962–65	UCLA	def. back
	Detroit Lions	1965–66		
Carver Shannon	Los Angeles Rams	1962–64	Southern Illinois	def. back
Art Perkins	Los Angeles Rams	1962–63	North Texas St.	fullback
John Brown	Cleveland Browns	1962–66	Syracuse	off. tackle
	Pittsburgh Steelers	1967–71		
	Injured	1972		

Player	*Team*	*Years*	*School*	*Position*
Sam Tidmore	Cleveland Browns	1962–63	Ohio State	linebacker
Johnny Counts	New York Giants	1962–63	Illinois	halfback
Bennie McRae	Chicago Bears	1962–70	Michigan	def. back
	New York Giants	1971		
Ron Hatcher	Washington Redskins	1962	Michigan St.	def. back
Leroy Jackson	Washington Redskins	1962–63	Western Illinois	halfback
Charley Frazier	Houston Oilers	1962–68	Texas Southern	receiver
	Boston Patriots	1969–70		
Booker Edgerson	Buffalo Bills	1962–69	Western Illinois	def. back
	Denver Broncos	1970		
Cookie Gilchrist	Buffalo Bills	1962–64	None	fullback
	Denver Broncos	1965		
	Miami Dolphin	1966		
	Denver Broncos	1967		
Ernie Warlick	Buffalo Bills	1962–65	N. Car. Central	def. end
Hezekiah Braxton	San Diego Chargers	1962	Virginia Union	fullback
	Buffalo Bills	1963		
Bobby Jackson	San Diego Chargers	1962–63	N Mexico St.	fullback
	Houston Oilers	1964		
	Oakland Raiders	1964		
	Houston Oilers	1965		
Jerry Robinson	San Diego Chargers	1962–64	Grambling	receiver
	New York Jets	1965		
Frank Buncom	San Diego Charger	1962–67	USC	linebacker
	Cincinnati Bengals	1968		
	(died September 14, 1969—pulmonary embolism)			
Donnie Davis	Dallas Texans	1962	Southern U.	flanker/
	Houston Oilers	1970		tight end
Curtis McClinton	Dallas Texans	1962	Kansas	fullback/
	Kansas City Chiefs	1963–69		tight end

*documented evidence shows that he was paid for the 1904 season, although recent evidence suggests that the Shelby Athletic Club was professional as early as 1902.
**played one game November 28, 1915

Notes

NOTES TO CHAPTER ONE

1. See Steven A. Riess, *Sport in Industrial America 1850–1920* (Wheeling, Ill.: Harlan Davidson, 1995).

2. Arthur R. Ashe, *A Hard Road to Glory* (New York: Warner Books, 1988), 47–70; Rick Wolff, ed., *The Baseball Encyclopedia* (New York: Macmillan, 1993), 1581–83.

3. Elliott J. Gorn and Warren Goldstein, *A Brief History of American Sports* (New York: Hill and Wang, 1993), 131, 155.

4. Ibid., 155.

5. Edna Rust and Art Rust Jr., *Illustrated History of the Black Athlete* (New York: Doubleday, 1985), 226.

6. Ibid., 226–27.

7. Ashe, *A Hard Road to Glory*, 90–91.

8. Ibid., 91–93.

9. Michael Hurd, *Black College Football 1892–1992* (Virginia Beach, Va.: Donning Company, 1993), 10.

10. Ibid., 12–13; Earl H. Duval, Jr., "An Historical Analysis of the Central Intercollegiate Athletic Association and Its Influence on the Development of Black Intercollegiate Athletics: 1912–1984," Ph.D. dissertation, Kent State University, 1985, 24–25.

11. Gorn and Goldstein, *A Brief History of American Sports*, 132; Jerold Michael Strong, "The Emergence and Success of a Major League Professional Football Franchise in the San Francisco Bay Area," Ph.D. dissertation, University of Northern Colorado, 1991, 23.

12. Strong, "The Emergence and Success," 26–30; David S. Neft, Richard M. Cohen, and Rick Korch, *The Football Encyclopedia—The Complete Year-by-Year History of Professional Football from 1892 to the Present* (New York: St. Martin's Press, 1991), 17.

13. See National Football League, *The Official National Football League 1991 Record and Fact Book* (New York: Workman, 1991) for a general history of the NFL up to 1991; see also Marc S. Maltby, "The Origins and Early Development of Professional Football, 1890–1920," Ph.D. dissertation, Ohio University, 1987, an excellent history of pro football in Ohio.

14. Milton R. Roberts and John Seaburn, "The First Black Pro," *Akron Beacon Journal*, September 21, 1975.

15. Rust and Rust, *Illustrated History of the Black Athlete*, 227–28; Roberts and Seaburn, "The First Black Pro."

16. Rust and Rust, *Illustrated History of the Black Athlete*, 228–29.

17. Roberts and Seaburn, "The First Black Pro"; Jerry A. Acanfora, "A History of Black Professional Football Players from 1900–1946," 3. Paper located at Pro Football Hall of Fame, Canton, Ohio, 1976.

18. *Shelby Daily Globe*, September 16, 1904.

19. Roberts and Seaburn, "The First Black Pro."

20. Ibid.

21. Ibid.

22. Ibid.

23. Ashe, *A Hard Road to Glory*, 11.

24. Peter Rowe, *American Football* (Enfield, Great Britain: Guinness, 1988), 9.

25. Ibid., 9–10; Neft, Cohen and Korch, *The Football Encyclopedia*, 18.

26. Ashe, *A Hard Road to Glory*, 11.

27. Ocania Chalk, *Pioneers of Black Sport* (New York: Dodd, Mead and Company, 1975), 212.

28. Ibid.

29. Ibid.

30. Douglas A. Noverr and Lawrence E. Ziewacz, *The Games They Played: Sports in American History, 1865–1980* (Chicago: Nelson-Hall, 1983), 49.

NOTES TO CHAPTER TWO

1. John M. Carroll, *Fritz Pollard* (Urbana: University of Illinois Press, 1992), 178–79.

2. Ibid., 179.

3. Arthur R. Ashe, *A Hard Road to Glory* (New York: Warner Books, 1988), 99; Ocania Chalk, *Pioneers of Black Sport* (New York: Dodd, Mead and Company, 1975), 215–16.

4. Edna Rust and Art Rust, Jr., *Illustrated History of the Black Athlete* (New York: Doubleday, Inc., 1985), 231–32.

5. Ashe, *A Hard Road to Glory*, 14.

6. Rust and Rust, *Illustrated History of the Black Athlete*, 232.

7. Ocania Chalk, *Black College Sport* (New York: Dodd, Mead and Company, 1976), 172; Rust and Rust, *Illustrated History of the Black Athlete*, 232.

8. G. D. Clay, "First, There Was Fritz: Long before Art Shell, Pollard Was NFL's Pioneer Black Coach," *New York Newsday*, December 20, 1989, 129; Carroll, *Fritz Pollard*, 87–88.

9. Carroll, *Fritz Pollard*, 129.

10. Ibid., 111.

11. Ibid., 113.

12. David Levering Lewis, *W. E. B. Du Bois* (New York: Henry Holt, 1993), 529–30.

13. Carroll, *Fritz Pollard*, 121–22.

14. Ashe, *A Hard Road to Glory*, 12.

15. Martin Bauml Duberman, *Paul Robeson* (New York: Alfred A. Knopf, 1989), 19–20.

16. Ibid., 20.

17. Ibid.

18. Clay, "First, There Was Fritz," 129; Carroll, *Fritz Pollard*, 131–32.

19. National Football League, *75 Seasons—The Complete Story of the National Football League 1920–1995* (Atlanta: Turner Publishing, 1994), 24.

20. Carroll, *Fritz Pollard*, 143.

21. Ibid., 147–48.

22. Chalk, *Pioneers of Black Sport*, 220.

23. Ibid.

24. Duberman, *Paul Robeson*, 34.

25. Chalk, *Pioneers of Black Sport*, 222.

26. National Football League, *75 Seasons*, 30.

27. Ibid., 20.

28. Ibid., 32–33.

29. Ibid., 33.

30. Ibid.

31. Carroll, *Fritz Pollard*, 178.

32. Chalk, *Pioneers of Black Sport*, 223; Ashe, *A Hard Road to Glory*, 31–32.

33. Ashe, *A Hard Road to Glory*, 32.

34. Chalk, *Black College Sport*, 190.

35. Ibid., 190–91.

36. Chalk, *Pioneers of Black Sport*, 226.

37. Ibid.

38. Ibid., 226; *Chicago Defender*, October 15, 1932.

39. Chalk, *Pioneers of Black Sport*, 227.

40. Ibid.

41. Ibid., 228.

42. *Chicago Defender*, December 10, 1932.

43. Thomas G. Smith, "Outside the Pale: The Exclusion of Blacks from the National Football League, 1934–1946," *Journal of Sport History* 15, no. 3 (winter 1988), 256.

44. Ibid.

45. Chalk, *Pioneers of Black Sport*, 228.

46. Ibid.

47. *Chicago Defender*, December 10, 1933.

48. Ibid.

49. Ibid.

50. Chalk, *Pioneers of Black Sport*, 230.

51. Smith, "Outside the Pale," 259.

52. Ibid., 256.

53. Ibid., 257–58.

54. Ibid., 257.

55. Ibid., 259; Carroll, *Fritz Pollard*, 144–45.

56. Gerald R. Gems, "Shooting Stars: The Rise and Fall of Blacks in Professional Football," *Professional Football Researchers' Association Annual*, 1988 (North Huntington, Pa.), 11–15.

NOTES TO CHAPTER THREE

1. Gerald R. Gems, "Shooting Stars: The Rise and Fall of Blacks in Professional Football," *Professional Football Researchers' Association Annual*, 1988 (North Huntington, Pa.), 12.

2. Thomas G. Smith, "Outside the Pale: The Exclusion of Blacks from the National Football League, 1934–1946," *Journal of Sport History* 15, no. 3 (winter 1988), 259–60; Edna Rust and Art Rust, Jr., *Illustrated History of the Black Athlete* (New York: Doubleday, 1985), 237.

3. Smith, "Outside the Pale," 260.

4. John M. Carroll, *Fritz Pollard* (Urbana: University of Illinois Press, 1992), 197; *Chicago Defender*, October 27, 1928.

5. *Chicago Defender*, December 14, 1935.

6. *New York Age*, October 26, 1935; Carroll, *Fritz Pollard*, 198.

7. Carroll, *Fritz Pollard*, 199–200.

8. Ibid., 200; *New York Amsterdam News*, November 23, 1935.

9. *Chicago Defender*, September 12, October 17, 1936.

10. Carroll, *Fritz Pollard*, 201–2.

11. Bob Gill and Tod Maher, "Not Only the Ball Was Brown: Black Players in Minor League Football, 1933–46," *The Coffin Corner* XI, no. 5 (spring 1989), 12.

12. J. Wayne Burrell, "Sports Whirl," *New York Amsterdam News*, July 30, 1938.

13. Carroll, *Fritz Pollard*, 203; *New York Amsterdam News*, July 30, 1938.

14. Gill and Maher, "Not Only the Ball Was Brown," 13.

15. *Chicago Defender*, November 4, 1939.

16. Gill and Maher, "Not Only the Ball Was Brown," 14.

17. Smith, "Outside the Pale," 261–62; Carroll, *Fritz Pollard*, 271.

18. Smith, "Outside the Pale," 262; Carroll, *Fritz Pollard*, 204. On black players in the 1930s at predominantly white colleges, see Arthur R. Ashe, Jr., *A Hard Road to Glory: A History of the African American Athlete, 1919–1945* (New York: Warner Books, 1988), and Ocania Chalk, *Black College Sport* (New York: Dodd, Mead, and Company, 1976).

19. Smith, "Outside the Pale," 261.

20. Ibid., 269; *Chicago Defender*, September 24, 1938.

21. Smith, "Outside the Pale," 269.

22. *Pittsburgh Courier*, October 1, 1938.

23. Ibid.

24. Ibid.

25. *Chicago Defender*, October 1, 1938.

26. *Chicago Defender*, September 23, October 7, November 4, 1939.

27. *Chicago Defender*, November 25, 1939.

28. *Chicago Defender*, December 11, 1937; Woody Strode and Sam Young, *Goal Dust* (Lanham, Md.: Madison Books, 1990), 69.

29. Strode and Young, *Goal Dust*, 52–54.

30. Smith, "Outside the Pale," 267; Strode and Young, *Goal Dust*, 94–95.

31. Strode and Young, *Goal Dust*, 96.

32. Ibid., 65.

33. Smith, "Outside the Pale," 268; *Pittsburgh Courier*, January 13, 1940.

34. *Chicago Defender*, September 7, 1940.

35. William A. Brewer, "Has Professional Football Closed the Door?" *Opportunity* 18 (December 1940), 376.

36. *Chicago Defender*, September 7, 1940.

37. *Chicago Defender*, September 21, 1940.

38. Mike Rathlet and Don R. Smith, *Their Deeds and Dogged Faith* (New York: Balsam Press, 1984), 209.

39. Strode and Young, *Goal Dust*, 108–11.

40. Ibid., 117.

41. Ibid., 89.

42. Ibid.

43. *Cleveland Call and Post*, September 6, 1941. For information on Robinson and the integration of major league baseball, see also Jules Tygiel, *Baseball's Great Experiment: Jackie Robinson and His Legacy* (New York: Vintage, 1983).

44. *Chicago Defender*, September 6, 1941.

45. National Football League, *75 Seasons—The Complete Story of the National Football League 1920–1995* (Atlanta: Turner Publishing, 1994), 67–68.

46. Strode and Young, *Goal Dust*, 124–28.

47. Ibid., 134.

48. Ibid., 135; Arnold Rampersad, *Jackie Robinson* (New York: Alfred A. Knopf, 1997), 109.

49. Rampersad, *Jackie Robinson*, 109.

50. Myron Cope, *The Game That Was: The Early Days of Pro Football* (New York: Vintage, 1970), 250; Smith, "Outside the Pale," 271.

51. Rust and Rust, *Illustrated History of the Black Athlete*, 244; Smith, "Outside the Pale," 273.

52. Smith, "Outside the Pale," 272–73; *Pittsburgh Courier*, January 27, 1945; Stanley Frank, "Buddy Totes the Ball," *Collier's* 118 (November 23, 1946), 21.

53. National Football League, *75 Seasons*, 72.

54. *Pittsburgh Courier*, February 17, 1945; *Baltimore Afro-American*, March 3, 1945; Smith, "Outside the Pale," 276.

55. Smith, "Outside the Pale," 275; Tygiel, *Baseball's Great Experiment*, 30.

56. Ocania Chalk, *Pioneers of Black Sport* (New York: Dodd, Mead, and Company, 1975), 78.

57. National Football League, *75 Seasons*, 72.

58. Smith, "Outside the Pale," 276.

59. Ibid., 276; *Pittsburgh Courier*, January 12, 1946.

60. Smith, "Outside the Pale," 276.

61. *Pittsburgh Courier*, January 26, 1946.

62. *Pittsburgh Courier*, February 2, 1946.

NOTES TO CHAPTER FOUR

1. John M. Carroll, *Fritz Pollard* (Urbana: University of Illinois Press, 1992), 214–15; William W. MacDonald, "The Black Athlete in American Sports," *Sports in Modern America*, ed. William J. Baker and John M. Carroll (St. Louis: River City Publishing, 1981), 97–98.

2. *Pittsburgh Courier*, March 30, 1946; Woody Strode and Sam Young, *Goal Dust* (Lanham, Md.: Madison Books, 1990), 141–42; Thomas G. Smith, "Outside the Pale: The Exclusion of Blacks from the National Football League, 1934–1946," *Journal of Sport History* 15, no. 3. (Winter 1988), 277.

3. *Pittsburgh Courier*, March 30, 1946.

4. Ibid.; *Baltimore Afro-American*, March 30, 1946; Smith, "Outside the Pale," 277.

5. Strode and Young, *Goal Dust*, 142.

6. Smith, "Outside the Pale," 277.

7. Paul Brown, with Jack Clary, *PB: The Paul Brown Story* (New York: Atheneum, 1979), 130.

8. Smith, "Outside the Pale," 277; Brown, with Clary, *PB: The Paul Brown Story*, 131.

9. Brown, with Clary, *PB: The Paul Brown Story*, 129.

10. Ibid., 129; Smith, "Outside the Pale," 277.

11. *Cleveland Call and Post*, August 17, 1946.

12. Contract between *Bill Willis* and the *Cleveland Franchise*, August 7, 1946, Archives, Pro Football Hall of Fame, Canton, Ohio; contract between *Marion Motley* and the *Cleveland Franchise*, August 10, 1946, Archives, Pro Football Hall of Fame, Canton, Ohio; contract between *Otto Graham, Jr.* and the *Cleveland Franchise*, March 28, 1945, Archives, Pro Football Hall of Fame, Canton, Ohio; contract between *Louis R. Groza* and the *Cleveland Franchise*, April 16, 1945, Archives, Pro Football Hall of Fame, Canton, Ohio; contract between *Dante Lavelli* and the *Cleveland Franchise*, December 27, 1945, Archives, Pro Football Hall of Fame, Canton, Ohio; contract between *Frank Gatski* and the *Cleveland Franchise*, February 5, 1946, Archives, Pro Football Hall of Fame, Canton, Ohio.

13. Strode and Young, *Goal Dust*, 148.

14. Ibid., 150.

15. Ibid., 151–52.

16. Ibid., 152.

17. Ibid., 150.

18. Ibid., 153–54.

19. *Los Angeles Sentinel*, November 14, 1946; National Football League, *75 Seasons—The Complete Story of the National Football League 1920–1995* (Atlanta: Turner Publishing, 1994), 75.

20. *Los Angeles Sentinel*, November 14, 1946; AAFC, *1949 Record Manual Supplement*, in Archives, Pro Football Hall of Fame, Canton, Ohio, 84.

21. *Cleveland Call and Post*, September 14, 1946; AAFC, *1949 Record Manual Supplement*, 84.

22. *Cleveland Call and Post*, September 14, 1946.

23. *Cleveland Call and Post*, September 14, September 21, 1946.

24. *Cleveland Call and Post*, September 21, 1946.

25. David S. Neft, Richard M. Cohen, and Rick Korch, *The Football Encyclopedia—The Complete Year-by-Year History of Professional Football from 1892 to the Present* (New York: St. Martin's Press, 1991), 191–95.

26. Brown, with Clary, *PB: The Paul Brown Story*, 129.

27. *Cleveland Call and Post*, November 23, 1946.

28. Smith, "Outside the Pale," 279–80.

29. *Cleveland Call and Post*, April 6, 1946.

NOTES TO CHAPTER FIVE

1. John M. Carroll, *Fritz Pollard* (Urbana: University of Illinois Press, 1992), 215–16.

2. *Cleveland Call and Post,* January 11, 1947.

3. Ibid.; *Los Angeles Sentinel,* January 9, 1947.

4. *Los Angeles Sentinel,* January 9, 1947; *New Jersey Afro-American,* January 25, February 1, 1947; *Pittsburgh Courier,* January 25, 1947.

5. *Cleveland Call and Post,* February 8, 1947; *New Jersey Afro-American,* April 26, 1947.

6. *New Jersey Afro-American,* April 26, 1947.

7. Ibid.

8. Ibid.

9. *New Jersey Afro-American,* August 16, 1947; *Los Angeles Sentinel,* July 31, September 4, 1947.

10. Woody Strode, and Sam Young, *Goal Dust* (Lanham: Md.: Madison Books, 1990), 155.

11. Ibid., 155; Alexander Wolff and Richard O' Brien, "Forgotten Pioneer," *Sports Illustrated* 82, no. 2 (January 16, 1995), 10–11.

12. *Chicago Defender,* October 25, 1947.

13. David S. Neft, Richard M. Cohen, and Rick Korch, *The Football Encyclopedia—The Complete Year-by-Year History of Professional Football from 1892 to the Present* (New York: St. Martin's Press, 1991), 191.

14. *New Jersey Afro-American,* August 30, 1947.

15. *Chicago Defender,* August 23, 1947.

16. *Los Angeles Sentinel,* March 20, 1947.

17. Neft, Cohen, and Korch, *The Football Encyclopedia,* 204; *Los Angeles Sentinel,* September 18, 1947.

18. Neft, Cohen, and Korch, *The Football Encyclopedia,* 205; *Los Angeles Sentinel,* December 4, 1947.

19. Neft, Cohen, and Korch, *The Football Encyclopedia,* 205.

20. All-America Football Conference, *1949 Record Manual Supplement,* in Archives, Pro Football Hall of Fame, Canton, Ohio, 84.

21. *Cleveland Call and Post,* October 11, 1947.

22. *New Jersey Afro-American,* April 10, 1948; *African-Americans In Pro Football,* in Archives, Pro Football Hall of Fame, Canton, Ohio, 27.

23. *African-Americans,* Archives, Pro Football Hall of Fame, 28.

24. *Los Angeles Sentinel,* November 18, 1948; AAFC, *1949 Record Manual Supplement,* 84.

25. *Cleveland Call and Post,* December 25, 1948; Neft, Cohen, and Korch, *The Football Encyclopedia,* 209.

26. Michael Hurd, *Black College Football 1892–1992* (Virginia Beach, Va.: Donning Company, 1993), 118–19.

27. *Cleveland Call and Post*, December 10, 1949.

28. Ibid.

29. Ibid.

30. Ibid.

NOTES TO CHAPTER SIX

1. See David S. Neft, Richard M. Cohen, and Rick Korch, *The Football Encyclopedia—The Complete Year-by-Year History of Professional Football from 1892 to the Present* (New York: St. Martin's Press, 1991); see also National Football League, *75 Seasons—The Complete Story of the National Football League 1920–1995* (Atlanta: Turner Publishing, 1994).

2. *Cleveland Call and Post*, July 15, 1950.

3. *Chicago Defender*, September 9, 1950.

4. Ibid.

5. Ibid.

6. *Chicago Defender*, September 9, 1950; *Michigan Chronicle*, September 11, 1950.

7. *Chicago Defender*, September 9, 1950.

8. *Chicago Defender*, November 11, 1950; *New Jersey Afro-American*, November 11, 1950.

9. *New Jersey Afro-American*, October 7, 1950.

10. Ibid.

11. Ibid.

12. Ibid.

13. Ibid.

14. *Cleveland Call and Post*, September 22, 1951.

15. National Football League, *75 Seasons*, 103; *Cleveland Call and Post*, January 26, 1952.

16. *New Jersey Afro-American*, January 26, 1952.

17. Ibid.

18. *Los Angeles Sentinel*, July 3, 1952, 6.

19. *Chicago Defender*, November 29, 1952.

20. Ibid.

21. National Football League, *75 Seasons*, 103–4; *New Jersey Afro-American*, January 17, 1953.

22. *Chicago Defender*, November 29, 1952.

23. Ibid.

24. Ocania Chalk, *Pioneers of Black Sport* (New York: Dodd, Mead and Company, 1975), 240.

25. *New Jersey Afro-American,* October 17, 1953.

26. *Michigan Chronicle,* September 10, 1955.

27. Chalk, *Pioneers of Black Sport,* 242.

28. *Cleveland Call and Post,* November 26, 1955; Paul Brown, with Jack Clary, *PB: The Paul Brown Story* (New York: Atheneum, 1979), 239.

29. Jim Brown, with Steve Delsohn, *Out of Bounds* (New York: Kensington Publishing Corp., 1989), 47, 55.

30. Ibid., 55–56.

31. *New Jersey Afro-American,* January 12, 1957.

32. *New Jersey Afro-American,* February 2, 1957.

33. *New Jersey Afro-American,* February 9, 1957.

34. *New Jersey Afro-American,* October 19, October 26, 1957.

35. Roosevelt Grier, *Rosey: An Autobiography* (Tulsa, Okla.: Harrison House, 1986), 131.

36. *New Jersey Afro-American,* October 18, 1958.

37. *New Jersey Afro-American,* November 1, 1958.

38. *New Jersey Afro-American,* November 8, 1958.

39. *New Jersey Afro-American,* October 25, November 29, 1958.

40. Brown, with Delsohn, *Out of Bounds,* 80.

41. *New Jersey Afro-American,* January 24, 1959.

NOTES TO CHAPTER SEVEN

1. Thomas G. Smith, "Civil Rights on the Gridiron: The Kennedy Administration and the Desegregation of the Washington Redskins," *Journal of Sport History* 14, no. 2 (summer 1987), 189–90.

2. Ibid., 191; George Sullivan, *Pro Football's All-Time Greats: The Immortals in Pro Football's Hall of Fame* (New York: Henry Holt, 1968), 79.

3. Tex Maule, "The Shaky New League," *Sports Illustrated* 12, no. 4 (January 25, 1960), 49–50.

4. *Houston Informer,* August 20, 1960.

5. Ibid.

6. *Houston Informer,* September 24, October 15, 1960.

7. *Houston Informer,* September 10, 1960.

8. Smith, "Civil Rights on the Gridiron," 194–95.

9. Ibid., 194–95; Chuck Stone, "Are D.C. Colored People Making Any Progress?" *Baltimore Afro-American,* May 20, 1961; David Lawrence, "The Nation's Capital: A Troubled City," *U.S. News and World Report* 48 (April 4, 1960), 84–85.

10. *Chicago Defender*, October 8, 1960.

11. *Chicago Defender*, November 5, 1960.

12. Smith, "Civil Rights on the Gridiron," 195; *Baltimore Afro-American*, October 8, 22, November 26, 1960, January 14, 1961; *Washington Post*, December 20, 29, 1960.

13. Smith, "Civil Rights on the Gridiron," 197.

14. Ibid., 197–200.

15. Ibid., 199–200; *Washington Post*, March 26, 1961; *Pittsburgh Courier*, April 22, 1961.

16. *New Jersey Afro-American*, August 5, 1961.

17. *New Jersey Afro-American*, August 12, 1961.

18. *New Jersey Afro-American*, August 19, 26, 1961.

19. *New Jersey Afro-American*, September 2, 1961.

20. Smith, "Civil Rights on the Gridiron," 201.

21. David Harris, *The League: The Rise and Decline of the NFL* (New York: Vintage, 1986), 145; *Washington Post*, September 12, 1962; Smith, "Civil Rights on the Gridiron," 202–3.

22. Smith, "Civil Rights on the Gridiron," 203.

23. *New Jersey Afro-American*, November 11, 1961.

24. David S. Neft, Richard M. Cohen, and Rick Korch, *The Football Encyclopedia—The Complete, Year-by-Year History of Professional Football from 1892 to the Present* (New York: St. Martin's Press, 1991), 335.

25. *Washington Post*, December 10, 1961; *Baltimore Afro-American*, December 23, 1961; Smith, "Civil Rights on the Gridiron," 204.

26. *Sporting News*, December 27, 1961; *Washington Post*, December 15, 1961; *Pittsburgh Courier*, December 30, 1961; *Baltimore Afro-American*, December 30, 1961; Smith, "Civil Rights on the Gridiron," 204.

27. Paul Fine, "Historically Speaking," *Black Sports* 7, no. 7 (January 1978), 59.

28. Ibid.

29. Smith, "Civil Rights on the Gridiron," 207.

30. *New Jersey Afro-American*, September 8, 1962.

31. Tex Maule, "The Redskins Find a New Kick—Winning," *Sports Illustrated* 17 (October 15, 1962), 61–63; *Washington Post*, September 24, October 8, 1962; *Pittsburgh Courier*, October 6, 1962; Smith, "Civil Rights on the Gridiron," 207.

32. Smith, "Civil Rights on the Gridiron," 207.

33. Fine, "Historically Speaking," 61.

34. Ibid., 60.

Bibliography

NEWSPAPERS

The Afro-American Newspaper (New York, New York)
The Atlanta Daily World (Atlanta, Georgia)
The Birmingham Reporter (Birmingham, Alabama)
The Chicago Defender (Chicago, Illinois)
Chicago Tribune (Chicago, Illinois)
The Cleveland Call and Post (Cleveland, Ohio)
Cleveland Plain Dealer (Cleveland, Ohio)
The Houston Informer (Houston, Texas)
The Indianapolis Freeman (Indianapolis, Indiana)
The Los Angeles Sentinel (Los Angeles, California)
The Los Angeles Times (Los Angeles, California)
The Los Angeles Tribune (Los Angeles, California)
Massillon Independence (Massillon, Ohio)
Michigan Chronicle (Detroit, Michigan)
Milwaukee Journal (Milwaukee, Wisconsin)
New Jersey Afro-American (Newark, New Jersey)
New York Daily News (New York, New York)
Pittsburgh Courier (Pittsburgh, Pennsylvania)
The Shelby Daily Globe (Shelby, Ohio)
Toledo Evening News Bee (Toledo, Ohio)
Washington Post (Washington, D.C.)

BOOKS

Ashe, Arthur, R. *A Hard Road to Glory*. New York: Warner Books, 1988.
Bennett, Lerone, Jr. *Before the Mayflower*. New York: Penguin Books, 1982.
———. *Wade in the Water: Great Moments in Black History*. Chicago: Johnson Publishing Company, 1979.
Billings, Robert. *Pro Football Digest*. Chicago: Follett Publishing Company, 1973.
Braunwart, Bob, and Bob Carroll. *The Alphabet Wars: The Birth of Professional Football, 1890–1892*. North Huntington, Pa.: Professional Football Researchers' Association, 1981.
Brown, Gene. *The Complete Book of Football*. New York: Arno Press, 1980.
Brown, Jim. *Off My Chest*. New York: Doubleday, 1964.
Brown, Jim, with Steve Delsohn. *Out of Bounds*. New York: Kensington Publishing Corp., 1989.

Brown, Paul, with Jack Clary. *PB: The Paul Brown Story*. New York: Atheneum, 1979.

Camp, Walter. *American Football*. New York: Arno Press [1898], 1974.

Carroll, John M. *Fritz Pollard*. Urbana: University of Illinois Press, 1992.

Chalk, Ocania. *Black College Sport*. New York: Dodd, Mead, and Company, 1976.

———. *Pioneers of Black Sport*. New York: Dodd, Mead, and Company, 1975.

Claassen, Harold. *Football's Unforgettable Games*. New York: Ronald Press, 1960.

———. *The History of Professional Football*. Upper Saddle River, N.J.: Prentice-Hall, 1963.

———. *The Ronald Encyclopedia of Football*. New York: Ronald Press, 1960.

Daley, Arthur. *Pro Football's Hall of Fame: The Official Book*. Chicago: Quadrangle Books, 1963.

Danzig, Allison. *History of American Football*. Upper Saddle River, N.J.: Prentice-Hall, 1956.

Duberman, Martin Bauml. *Paul Robeson*. New York: Alfred A. Knopf, 1989.

Dulles, Foster Rhea. *A History of Recreation: America Learns to Play*. New York: Appleton-Crofts, 1965.

Durso, Joseph. *The All-American Dollar: The Big Business of Sports*. Boston: Houghton-Mifflin, 1971.

Edwards, Harry. *Sociology of Sports*. Homewood, Ill.: Dorsey Press, 1973.

Figler, Stephen, K. *Sport and Play in American Life: A Textbook in the Sociology of Sport*. Philadelphia: Saunders College Publishers, 1981.

Foner, Philip, S. *Paul Robeson Speaks: Writings, Speeches and Interviews*. London: Quartette Books, 1978.

Grier, Roosevelt. *Rosey: An Autobiography*. Tulsa, Okla.: Harrison House, 1986.

Hamilton, Virginia. *Paul Robeson: The Life and Times of a Free Black Man*. New York: Harper and Row, 1974.

Hurd, Michael. *Black College Football 1892–1992*. Virginia Beach, Va.: Donning Company, 1993.

Isaac, Stan. *Jim Brown: The Golden Year 1964*. Upper Saddle River, N.J.: Prentice-Hall, 1970.

Johnson, Chuck. *The Green Bay Packers*. New York: Thomas Nelson and Sons, 1961.

Jones, Wally, and Jim Washington. *Black Champions Challenge American Sports*. New York: David McKay Company, 1972.

Kaye, Ivan N. *Good Clean Violence: A History of College Football*. Philadelphia: Lippincott, 1973.

Klein, Dave. *The New York Giants: Yesterday, Today, Tomorrow.* Chicago: Regnery, 1971.

Klosinski, Emil. *Pro Football in the Days of Rockne.* New York: Carlton Press, 1970.

Krout, John Allen. *Annals of American Sport.* New Haven: Yale University Press, 1929.

Leckie, Robert. *The Story of Football.* New York: Random House, 1965.

Lucas, John A., and Ronald A. Smith. *The Saga of American Sport.* Philadelphia: Lea and Febiger, 1978.

March, Harry, A. *Pro Football, Its "Ups" and "Downs."* Albany, N.Y.: J. B. Lyon Company, 1934.

Mason, Nicholas. *Football! The Story of All the World's Football Games.* New York: Drake Publishers, 1975.

Maule, Hamilton "Tex." *The Game: The Official Picture History of the NFL and AFL.* New York: Random House, 1967.

Michael, Paul. *Professional Football's Greatest Games.* Upper Saddle River, N.J.: Prentice-Hall, 1972.

Morris, Willie. *The Courting of Marcus Dupree.* Garden City, N.Y.: Doubleday, 1983.

Names, Larry, D. *The History of the Green Bay Packers: The Lambeau Years, Part One.* Wautoma, Wis.: Angel Press of Wisconsin, 1987.

National Football League. *The Official National Football League 1991 Record and Fact Book.* New York: Workman, 1991.

————. *75 Seasons—The Complete Story of the National Football League 1920–1995.* Atlanta: Turner Publishing, 1994.

Neft, David S., Richard M. Cohen, and Rick Korch. *The Football Encyclopedia—The Complete Year-by-Year History of Professional Football from 1892 to the Present.* New York: St. Martin's Press, 1991.

Noverr, Douglas A. and Lawrence E. Ziewacz. *The Games They Played: Sports in American History, 1865–1980.* Chicago: Nelson-Hall, 1983.

Peterson, James A. *Slater of Iowa.* Chicago: Hinkley and Schmitt, 1958.

Peterson, Robert. *Only the Ball Was White: A History of Legendary Black Players and All-Black Professional Teams.* New York: McGraw-Hill [1970], 1984.

Powel, Harford. *Walter Camp, the Father of American Football: An Authorized Biography.* Freeport, N.Y.: Books for Libraries Press [1926], 1970.

Riess, Steven A., ed. *The American Sporting Experience: A Historical Anthology of Sport in America.* New York: Leisure Press, 1984.

Riffenburgh, Beau, ed. *The Official NFL Encyclopedia.* New York: New American Library, 1986.

Rogosin, Donn. *Invisible Men: Life in Baseball's Negro Leagues.* New York: Atheneum, 1985.

Rosenthal, Harold. *Fifty Faces of Football.* New York: Atheneum, 1981.

Rowe, Peter. *American Football.* Enfield, Great Britain: Guinness Publishing, 1988.

Rust, Edna, and Art Rust, Jr. *Illustrated History of the Black Athlete.* New York: Doubleday, 1985.

Smith, Robert. *Illustrated History of Pro Football.* New York: Grossett and Dunlap, 1977.

———. *Pro Football: The History of the Game and the Great Players.* Garden City, N.Y.: Doubleday, 1963.

The Sporting News 1986 Pro Football Yearbook. St. Louis: Sporting News Publishing Company, 1986.

Strode, Woody, and Sam Young. *Goal Dust.* Lanham, Md.: Madison Books, 1990.

Sullivan, George. *Pro Football's All-Time Greats: The Immortals in Pro Football's Hall of Fame.* New York: Henry Holt, 1968.

Tygiel, Jules. *Baseball's Great Experiment.* New York: Oxford University Press, 1983.

Vass, George. *George Halas and the Chicago Bears.* Chicago: Regnery, 1971.

Weyand, Alexander. *Football Immortals.* New York: Macmillan, 1962.

Wolff, Rick, ed. *The Baseball Encyclopedia.* New York: Macmillan, 1993.

Young, A. S. "Doc." *Negro Firsts in Sports.* Chicago: Johnson Publishing Company, 1963.

ARTICLES

Adelman, Melvin L. "Academicians and American Athletics: A Decade of Progress," *Journal of Sport History* 10 (Spring 1983), 80–106.

Boyle, Robert H. "All Alone by the Telephone," *Sports Illustrated* 7., no. 13 (October 16, 1961), 37–43.

Braunwart, Bob. and Bob Carroll. "Columbus Panhandles," *The Coffin Corner* 1 (October 1979), 1–7.

———. "The Rock Island Independents," *The Coffin Corner* 5 (March 1983), 3–6.

Captain, Gwendolyn. "Enter Ladies and Gentlemen of Color: Gender, Sport, and the Ideal of African American Manhood and Womanhood during the Late Nineteenth and Early Twentieth Centuries," *Journal of Sport History* 18, no. 1 (spring 1991), 81–102.

Carroll, Bob. "Akron Pros, 1920," *The Coffin Corner* 4 (December 1982), 7–8.

Clay, G. D. "First, There Was Fritz: Long before Art Shell, Pollard Was NFL's Pioneer Black Coach," *New York Newsday* (December 20, 1989), 129–35.

Edwards, Harry. "The Black 'Dumb Jock,' an American Sports Tragedy," *The College Board Review* 131 (spring 1984), 8–12.

Evans, Art. "Joe Louis as a Key Functionary: White Reactions toward a Black Champion," *Journal of Black Studies* 16, no. 1 (September 1985), 95–111.

Fidler, Douglas K., George Coroneos, and Michael Tamburro. "Frederick Jackson Turner, The Revisionists, and Sports Historiography," *Journal of Sport History* 2, no. 1 (spring 1985), 41–49.

Fine, Paul. "Historically Speaking," *Black Sports* 7, no. 7 (January 1978), 57–61.

Gill, Bob, and Ted Maher. "Not Only the Ball Was Brown: Black Players in Minor League Football, 1933–46," *The Coffin Corner* XI, no. 5 (spring 1989), 12–14.

Maule, Hamilton "Tex". "The Shaky New League," *Sports Illustrated* 12, no. 4 (January 25, 1960), 49–53.

Roberts, Milton R., and John Seaburn. "The First Black Pro," *Akron Beacon Journal*, (September 21, 1975), 4D–6D.

Smith, Thomas G. "Civil Rights on the Gridiron: The Kennedy Administration and the Desegregation of the Washington Redskins," *Journal of Sport History* 14, no. 2 (summer 1987), 189–208.

———. "Outside the Pale: The Exclusion of Blacks from the National Football League, 1934–1946," *Journal of Sport History* 15, no. 3 (winter 1988), 255–281.

Spivey, Donald. "End Jim Crow in Sports: The Protest at New York University, 1940–1941," *Journal of Sport History* 15, no. 3 (winter 1988), 282–303.

Wiggins, David K. "From Plantation to Playing Field: Historical Writings on the Black Athlete in American Sport," *Research Quarterly for Exercise and Sport* 57, no. 2 (1986), 101–16.

———. "The 1936 Olympic Games in Berlin: The Response of America's Black Press," *Research Quarterly for Exercise and Sport* 54, no. 3. (1983), 278–92.

———. "The Play of Slave Children in the Plantation Communities of the Old South, 1820–1860," *Journal of Sport History* 7, no. 2 (summer 1980), 21–39.

———. "Wendell Smith, the *Pittsburgh Courier-Journal* and the Campaign to Include Blacks in Organized Baseball, 1933–1945," *Journal of Sport History* 10, no. 2 (summer 1983), 5–29.

Wolff, Alexander, and Richard O'Brien. "Forgotten Pioneer," *Sports Illustrated* 82, no. 2 (January 16, 1995), 10–11.

UNPUBLISHED MATERIALS

Adelman, Melvin L. "An Assessment of Sports History Theses in the United States, 1931–1976, " M.S. Thesis, University of Illinois, 1970.

Borkowski, Richard P. "The Life and Contributions of Walter Camp to American Football," Ph.D. dissertation, Temple University, 1979.

Brower, Jonathan Jacob. "The Black Side of Football: The Salience of Race," Ph.D. dissertation, University of California, Santa Barbara, 1972.

Burns, Clarence Eugene. "Position Occupancy Patterns as a Function of Race: The National Football League Draft, 1968 to 1983," Ph.D. dissertation, University of Montana, 1988.

Duval, Earl H., Jr. "An Historical Analysis of the Central Intercollegiate Athletic Association and Its Influence on the Development of Black Intercollegiate Athletics: 1912–1984," Ph.D. dissertation, Kent State University, 1985.

Frommer, Harvey. "A Description of How Professional Football Employed the Medium of Television to Increase the Sport's Economic Growth and Cultural Impact, 1960–1970," Ph.D. dissertation, New York University, 1974.

Maltby, Marc S. "The Origins and Early Development Of Professional Football, 1890–1920," Ph.D. dissertation, Ohio University, 1987.

Strong, Jerold Michael. "The Emergence and Success of a Major League Professional Football Franchise in the San Francisco Bay Area," Ph.D. dissertation, University of Northern Colorado, 1991.

Index

Akron Indians, 14; signing of Fritz Pollard, 31
Akron Pros, 31–33
All-American Football Conference, 75, 77, 100, 111–112; All-Star game, 115–116; attendance during 1946 season, 90–92; integration of, 86
Allegheny Athletic Association, 9
American Football League (1926), 35–36
American Football League (1959), 140–141, 144; and black players, 149; creation of, 140–141
American Professional Football Association (APFA), 61; formation of league, 61

Baker, Charles "Doc," 14
Bass, Bill, 106–107
Brackins, Charles, 133; as black quarterback with Green Bay Packers, 133
Bradley, Harold, 37; and the Chicago Cardinals, 37
Briscoe, Marlin, 160
Brown, Jim, 134–135, 139
Brown, Paul, 73, 84, 95
Brown Bombers, 52–55
Butler, Sol, 22, 34

Camp, Walter, 5, 6, 7
Canton Bulldogs, 15
Chattanooga Ramblers, 52
Chicago American Giants, 54
Chicago Black Hawks, 51–52
Chicago Comets, 57
Chicago Defender, 39–41; and Dallas Texans, 129
Civil Rights Act of 1875, 7

Dallas Texans, 128–130

Fletcher, Ollie "Art," 125–126; and Baltimore Colts, 126
Flippin, George A., 7
Follis, Charles W., 10, 11, 12; as first black pro, 10
Fowler, J. W. "Bud," 4

Gates, William "Pop," 98; and the National Basketball League, 98
Gillom, Horace, 100, 109
Gillom, Joe, 161; and Pittsburgh Steelers, 161
Grange, Harold "Red," 34; and the AFL, 35, 43
Grier, Rosey, 137

Halas, George, 19, 32, 34; black All-Star game, 60; formation of NFL color barrier, 44–46
Harding, Halley, 78; and LA Coliseum Commission, 78
Harris, Elmore "Pepper," 102–103, 107
Harris, James, 161; and black quarterbacks, 161
Heffelfinger, Pudge, 10; as first professional football player, 10
Houston Informer, 144–145; and Houston Oilers, 144–145
Hudson, Dick, 34

Johnson, Jack, 4, 16–17

Kemp, Ray, 37; coaches black All-Stars, 60; member of Pittsburgh Pirates, 42; NFL release, 44
Kennedy, John F., 147–148; administrative changes as president, 147–148
King, William "Dolly," 98; and the National Basketball League, 98
Klep, Eddie, 97; as white member of Cleveland Buckeyes, 97

Lacy, Sam, 125, 148; and Baltimore Colts, 125; boycott of Redskins, 136, 138, 146; criticism of George Preston Marshall, 148–149
Lewis, William Henry, 6; as first black collegiate football player, 6
Lillard, Joe, 37; collegiate career, 38–39; and formation of color barrier, 44; joins APFA, 61; member of Brown Bombers, 53; member of Chicago Cardinals, 39

Lipscomb, Eugene "Big Daddy," 131; and endorsement of JFK, 147

Mann, Bob, 111; traded by Lions, 123–125
March Field Fliers, 71; and service teams during World War II, 71
Marshall, George Preston, 46, 50, 79, 131–132, 134, 143, 146, 158; and U.S. Secretary of Interior, 150–158
Marshall, Robert W., 23
Massillon Tigers, 12, 15
McDonald, Henry, 16
Mike, Robert, 111; release by 49ers, 122–123
Mitchell, Bobby, 155; integrates Redskins, 155–158
Motley, Marion, 73, 94, 109, 113; integrates AAFC, 85, 93–96; retirement, 133–134, 139
Murphy, Isaac, 3; and black jockeys, 3

National Association for the Advancement of Colored People (NAACP), 116; and AAFC All-Star Game, 116; Birmingham branch and NFL, 127; D.C. branch and NFL, 136; Norfolk branch and NFL, 152; Roanoke branch and NFL, 151–152
National Football League (NFL), 1, 19, 100, 112, 156–157, 160; creation of color barrier, 44–47, 79; decline of black players, 22, 33, 37; merger with AAFC, 120–121; and racial policies, 162–164; reintegration of, 82; and World War II, 70–71
Nisby, John, 155; integrates Redskins, 155–156
Northwest Football League (NWFL), 57; and black teams, 57

Pacific Coast League, 66; and Kenny Washington, 66–67
Pollard, Fritz, 23; collegiate career, 24–28; organizes black teams, 51–52; retirement, 36–37; signed by Akron Indians, 31

Rickey, Branch, 11, 12, 76
Robeson, Paul, 26; collegiate career, 27–31; signed by Akron Pros, 32
Robinson, Jackie, 11, 63, 67, 72, 76, 96; breaks into major league baseball, 102, 107; criticizes Boston Red Sox, 140
Rozelle, Pete, 151, 153; and George Preston Marshall, 153

Schlissler, Paul, 44; on coaching Joe Lillard, 44–45; founds PCL, 66
Schramm, Tex, 44
Shelbourne, John, 33; and Hammond Pros, 33
Shelby Athletic Club (Association), 10, 12
Simmons, Ozzie, 58–59; joins APFA, 61
Slater, Fred "Duke," 33, 36–37, 39; coaches black All-Stars, 60
Smith, Gideon E. "Charlie," 18
Strode, Woody, 63, 66; member of Hollywood Bears, 66–67; reintegrates NFL, 83, 88–90; release by LA Rams, 104

Taliaferro, George, 115, 128
Thorpe, Jim, 16, 32, 36
Thrower, Willie, 131; as black quarterback with Chicago Bears, 131
Tunnell, Emlen, 111, 139

Udall, Stewart L., 149–150, 153; and George Preston Marshall, 149–150

Virginia Negro League (VNL), 57–58; black professional football league, 57–58

Walker, Moses Fleetwood, 4
Washington, Kenny, 62–65, 105; member of Hollywood Bears, 67; reintegrates NFL, 82, 88–90; retirement, 112, 139
Washington Redskins, 130, 154–155; boycott of, 137; and 1957 draft, 134; and 1961 draft, 148; threatened boycott of, 130
Williams, Doug, 161–162; as black quarterback in Super Bowl, 161–162

Williams, Jay "Inky," 33–34

Willis, Bill, 73, 91, 109; integrates AAFC, 84–85, 93–96

Wismer, Harry, 136, 144; as minority owner of Redskins, 136

Young, Claude "Buddy," 74, 109; and College All-Stars, 106; member of Dallas Texans, 128; scout for Baltimore Colts, 139; signing of, 100–102

Younger, Paul "Tank," 114–115

About the Author

Charles K. Ross is an assistant professor of Afro-American studies and history at the University of Mississippi.